Moor Row
in 1891

Railway Town
Mining Plantation
Rural Dormitory

Dugald R Sperry Lamb

Published in 2023 by Dugald R Sperry Lamb

© Copyright Dugald R Sperry Lamb

Paperback version
ISBN: 978-1-913898-75-5

also available in Hardback

Cover and Book interior Design by Russell Holden
www.pixeltweakspublications.com

A Catalogue record for this book is available from the British Library.

Printed by IngramSpark

All rights reserved without limiting the rights under copyright reserved above, no parts of this publication may be reproduced, stored in or introduced into a retrieval system, or transmitted in any form, or by any means (electronic, mechanical, photocopying, recording or otherwise) without the prior written permission of Dugald R Sperry Lamb, the copyright owner and the publisher of this book.

For Molly.

Contents

Acknowledgements i
Introduction iii
Wild West Comes To The Moor 1
Britain's History In Moor Row 4
Normans, Monks, Cattle Thieves And Accountants. 18
Moor Row Was Once A Moor 24
Moor Row Residents 1891 Organised By Streets. 29
Living Memories Of Moor Row In 2021 83
Moor Row In Government Records 87
Making Money By Making Iron 91
Making Money With Land 93
Lowther's Luck 97
Trickle Down Of Money 101
Health And Safety At Work 112
The Best Way To Make Money Is To Have Rich Parents .. 114
Owners Combinations And Workers Associations 130
The Need For Railways 139
Moor Row Junction 143
Moor Row Hot Spots 149
Cumbria Industries 162
The History Of Moor Row's Future 169

Appendix
1. Naming Of Mines 179
2. Mines Within 5 Miles Of Moor Row 180
3. Notes On The Ownership Of Mines. 181
4. Mine Owning Companies In 1901 183
5. Major Cumberland Mining Areas 186
6. Family Seats Around Moor Row In 1829 188
7. The Row on the Moor as built in 1891 192
References 199

ACKNOWLEDGEMENTS

In 2020 residents of Moor Row and Britain were told to stop meeting up by their government and stay at home, to avoid catching the modern plague of COVID 19. Most people followed the instruction with varying amounts of alarm or alacrity, and occupied their free time with a variety of pastimes. One amusement in Moor Row was unpicking village myths that pre-dated the folk lore of peoples memories. Many thought Moor Row deserved a history all to itself based on sources that could be studied separately, rather than suppositions and stories. After all Cleator, Frizington, Arlecdon, Egremont and Whitehaven had their histories in print.

This book presents a history of a village using already published stuff to summarise things going on inside and outside Cumbria that made Moor Row out of cold clay fields.

Although it is about history, it is not a piece of historical research. It is a narrative put together from the work of historians. Neither is it been written by an historian. It was written by a student of chemistry and economics, who made a living as a scientist and one time tutor. It uses data from original government surveys and newspaper reports to shine light on the lives of Moor Row residents near the peak of its industrial boom and contrast their lives using vignettes with the lives of their bosses.

More research could be done on landownership in the area, perhaps on individual case studies of family growth and movements, if some others fancy the work. Such research would usefully add to the biography of the class of working folk who lived in Moor Row. There is plenty already written about the landowners who took such care to preserve their own histories.

This work was sustained with much encouragement throughout the planning, drafting and writing of this work. Special mention must be made of Henry Cook of Cobra Castle, Ralph Edmunds, Ted Biggins, and Francis Hill of Dalzell Street who each brought life and colour to the sepia prints posted on internet sites and newspaper articles. Harley Young, Sienna Young, Lexi May Willan are gratefully acknowledged for the questions they posed that served as the inspiration to turn ideas about Moor Row from 'the olden days' in to a book about Moor Row in a world contemplating fossil fuelled global climate change.

Thank you also to Velda Cook for reading drafts and patiently offering suggestions for improvement.

The errors in the book are all my own work.

INTRODUCTION

This is a story about the history of Moor Row, a Cumbria village which started to be built in 1850. Its history was not written as it happened, but was left to be set down after the dust has settled, using particular facts to make a preferred story entertaining. History might reveal patterns in behaviour and help make modern day decisions, and history may also be a way of reinforcing prejudices and ambitions. Hindsight can make events appear inevitable, as contemporary values are often lost or misunderstood by observers today. Looking at the past seldom recognises that the problems we face today are the answers to problems of years ago.

In 2022 it is claimed the three major worries the Government of London faces are (1) an overstretched welfare system, buckling from the effects of a COVID pandemic that was predicted in 2016; (2) an economy reeling from a European war in Ukraine that had been planned for since 1948, and (3) falling standards of living to due low wages and high inflation.

In West Cumbria, the weapons grade nuclear factory at Sellafield has closed threatening jobs in the latest round of cuts to work that started in the 1980s. In an age of national commitment to reduce carbon emissions to control climate changes to the world, the UK government has approved plans to build a brand new coal mine under Whitehaven. It is hard to see these outcomes were ever planned or anticipated, yet today they seem as inevitable as the sun rising tomorrow.

Two hundred years ago the imperative was to maintain control of a country at the centre of an empire spread across the world, that used steel production for projection of power and authority over the empire and its competitors. In the 1600s, the 1700s, and the early 1800s there had been attempts to make money from the buried wealth of Cumberland by its landowners. It was the invention of steam powered machines for heavy work for long periods that provided the key to a new future for the county. Workers became servants of machines, to feed them coal and water and raw materials. Many landowners exploited the new opportunities of industrialisation by welcoming the new machines, either as calculating rentiers or risk taking industrialists. There was no fundamental choice for owners between running industry or owning land, since many owners were already active entrepreneurs. Their caricature as either refined and genteel dynastic patricians or bucolic illiterate clod hoppers are misleading. The Duke of Norfolk, for instance, paid for the restoration and expansion of his castle at Arundel and repairs to the Cathedral with a portion of the profits from his Sheffield coal mines. The Chaloners of Guisborough in 1825 paid for their failed Wentworth, Chaloner and Rishworth bank using profits from new lead mines; The Marquess of Londonderry gambled his fortune on building a harbour at Seaham[1]; The Marquess of Stafford and the Earl of Ellesmere were both involved in increasing their wealth through involvement in collieries, canals, railways and manufacturing.

Victorian Cumberland of the 1800s covered 850,000 acres of land (3,500,000,000 square metres) and was owned by a few people, who each owned up to 50,000 acres as individuals. This cast of County families included the Ballantyne Dykes, Bradylls, Benns, Cavendishes, Christians, Curwens, Fletchers, Gales, Lawsons, Lamplughs, Leconfields, Lowthers, Pelhams, Percys, Ponsonbys, Penningtons, Scotts, Speddings, Senhouses to name a few. What held them back in the drive for improving their lives,

---

[1] Actually, Charles Vane the third Marquis Londonderry, had married Lady Frances Vane Tempest for her coal mines, and it was her money he spent on the harbour, also to build Wynyard Park mansion, and to restore Mount Stewart mansion in Ireland, and buy Holdernesse House on London's Park Lane.

and gave them a monopoly on local power, was the transport problems and communication difficulties of West Cumberland, that kept the area out of sight and mind of London's central powers.

The arrival of railways 20 years behind the rest of northern England opened up new places to send larger amounts of iron, steel, and coal once the landowners could see the benefits it would bring them. Until the railways made travelling efficient even the poets, rock climbers and painters who made the area famous usually visited by invitation or patronage of landowners.

Repeated government reports since the 1930s have concluded that West Cumbria is a neglected backwater of England, regardless of any modern day improvements in the education and welfare of the population. Without taking an historical interest in the region, the way events repeat themselves become lost to us. The Sellafield experience of contaminated land, contaminated beaches and contaminated river estuaries, is a repeat of how failing management of hereditary entrepreneurship still controls an isolated population until long after its best days. Once a business achieves a hold on local leadership it can supervise the exploitation of assets and draw them down in to a terminal decline with out resistance, and simultaneously claim to serve a philanthropic purpose [2]. Rather than benevolence, the behaviour is more like a mediaeval fiefdom.

In the early and mid twentieth century, and again in the twenty first century, the legacy for West Cumbria has been its perpetuation as a fringe district on the edge of a remote European county, left to cope with a slag heap of decaying industries and towns that day trippers can not be induced to visit, even in small numbers. Government funding using tax payers money, to retard the decline, has been limited to preparations for two world wars

---

[2] In 2020 the UK government declared disposal of radioactive waste did not need regulation if the death rate from waste was less than one person in a million. [Public Health England Centre for Radiation, Chemical and Environmental Hazards 'Assessing the risk to people's health from radioactive objects on beaches around the Sellafield site Summary Report' {2020} p10, Chilton, Didcot, Oxfordshire.

and an eternal cold war. In the 1990s there was an initiative to transform the area in to Britain's Energy Coast. Instead Cumbria got a Heritage Coast of old Royal Ordnance sites, at Eastriggs, Longtown, Broughton Moor, Blitterlees, Sellafield, Drigg, Barrow and the eleven redundant Royal Air Force stations along the coast. The current subsidised estates of light industry work shops and job creation schemes have failed to produce encouragement for the bright and talented to give up seeking their own fortunes elsewhere. This is the future for Moor Row written in its history. *Plus ça change, plus c'est la même chose!*

This essay started in debates about the origin of local street names, who was buried at the Quaker Bridge, and the type of jobs residents of the village had, to attempt to transform conjecture in to plausible explanations. Some of the answers come easily from archives and other histories, and references are included to help further study.

John Street was named after Sir John Walsh whose mine was at the end of the street. Penzance Street was named to honour Cornish immigrants of the 1850s diaspora: working in Cumberland mines was familiar to the Cornish miners who moved to the area as Cornish mines cut their work force. Or perhaps the name was chosen to tempt them to live and work in the area by using a familiar name for the street.

Scalegill Road goes to Scalegill, and School Street has schools on it. Railway Terrace was near the railway station and was built for railway workers. Church Street is on the footpath to St John's church in Bigrigg. The little street joining Church and John Streets is called William Street in some government records, and Dalzell Street is named after Thomas Henry, or John, or Anthony Dalzell who owned land along the road to Woodend formerly named Gutterby Lane. It is not likely to have been named for Dalzell the butcher who lived in Moor Row or Dalzell the brewer who had factories in Whitehaven and Cleator Moor.

The Quaker bridge was built on the site of a non-conformist cemetery beside Gutterby Lane in 'Sepulchre Meadow'. The cemetery and contents were moved when a railway bridge was built over it, and is commemorated with an inscribed stone on the bridge earth works in honour of a local Anabaptist minister.

Pearson was a local land owner who lived at the Montreal home stead near Galemire. Scalegill was also known once as Ingwell View. Postlethwaites mine was named for the Postlethwaite family of Hollins house in Whitehaven, who owned the land around what became known as Hollins Park. Gutterby was a country house, converted to workers cottages when mining started in the field behind.

There is no evidence of a fire brigade having been attached to Moor Row, much less a fire station serving the village, although there was a fire station in Cleator Moor on Quarry Road near Wyndham Street, close by the police station.

Moor Row and Scalegill grew from 25 homesteads to 300 households in the space of 100 years, becoming home to migrant labour from Ireland, main land England like Cornwall, Wales, the Isle of Man, Italy and Scotland as well as local Cumbrians. The first came to work the railway built to Rowrah from Whitehaven that served iron ore mines stretching between Egremont and Lamplugh. The mines supplied iron and steel works, to feed the growing ambition of Britain for knives, forks, ships, engines and weapons. The whole boom to bust cycle lasted 80 years, from about 1840 to 1920. By comparison, the more recent Sellafield nuclear factory was poured built about 1950, lasted about fifty years before its nuclear waste business was closed down and its boom days went bust.

CHAPTER 1

WILD WEST COMES TO THE MOOR

The sea is full of ships carrying the wealth of nations to feed and fuel the older countries that have over worked their own resources. Small undeveloped countries sell their grain, oil, metals and coal cheap. Two hundred years ago in the old rural county of Cumberland, iron ore was being dug up and shipped to ironworks in South Wales and Scotland. It was not until the end of the 1899 that shipments of ore from West Cumberland ports stopped. In the meantime, Victorian entrepreneurs had seen the possibility of iron and steel-making on a massive scale in the county and built furnaces to purify the ore and enrich themselves. So great was the scale of work that as the 1800s became the 1900s iron ore was being shipped in to Cumbria from countries which had neither the means nor the money to use the ore themselves. In the period 1830 to 1910, West Cumberland experienced a boom of money making that may never be seen again. The boom days are now history. What remains is a landscape scarred with spoil heaps,and large areas of flooded land sinking in to old mines, with a few terraces of cottages left in the villages that grew as quickly as the fortunes of Ironmasters.

These villages had a look of American western frontier towns gripped by a gold rush. The first flush of prosperity came gradually because mining of iron ore was labour-intensive, and West Cumberland did not have the manpower available to mine it on a large scale. That meant immigrants were needed from rural Britain, Ireland and Cornwall, skilled in hard rock mining in tin mines, ready for hard labour, to make a living to feed and clothe themselves. As ore mining grew, vast bodies of ore were found that linked up with other industries that grew around it. One of these industries was ore carrying on carts or horseback. Before the railways were built, hundreds of men and horses were used in the heavy traffic of carts and four-wheeled wagons. The golden age of making money started about 1870 when the railways had been built to most of the mines. Red iron grime from mines spilled across the countryside staining villages and hamlets, and the people. The iron ore was buried in a band of rocks about 14 miles long and up to three miles wide, between Rowrah and Egremont. Finding it required drilling a lot of holes in the ground, and the possibility of finding ore meant land was kept clear of buildings. Villages made up of single rows of houses sprang up along road sides, in what is called 'ribbon developments' that drive modern planners mad. Land owners were expecting fortunes to be made from ore bodies waiting to be found[1] under the fields.

For a very few people the area was rolling in prosperity. John Stirling was one of the big names of iron ore in Cumberland, and he made one of the largest fortunes out of it. He had leased the two Todholes farms in Cleator Moor, and set to work drilling for ore. He started the Todholes ore quarry, which took most of its vast output by cheap opencast working. Then Stirling took over the Montreal ground for mining. At one time the quarry and mine were digging up a quarter of a million tons of ore a year. Profit was the name of the game at all times. The mine manager ordered the undermining of the pit offices which sank in to the ground and were lost forever. Social services and public utilities could not keep pace with development. At the start of the boom there was practically no schooling available for children, most of whom were expected to start working at the age of ten, for six days a week and up to fourteen hours work each day.

---

[1] See Bulmers famous description of Frizington as 'one long street' [Bulmer 1901 p522]. Less famously, St Bees was described as one long street [Parson and White, 1829, p235]; Distington as one long street, p202; Drigg a long street of detached houses, p204; Egremont one wide street, p205, and Bootle as one short street, p178.

By the early 1880s the end to the golden days of the iron ore boom was approaching, as cheaper ore was found and new methods for making steel were invented. Demand for Cumbrian ore fell. To compete with the rest of the world, prices for Cumbrian ore were lowered and wages were cut for the miners. Unemployment rose, and with nothing but parish assistance to fall back on the miners had to look for work elsewhere. There was improvement in prices and work during war times with Cumbrian haematite in such demand that it was suggested Cleator Moor should be demolished to get to get to the haematite left underground holding the town up. The mine owners satisfied themselves by taking out columns of ore that held up the tunnels. Local Authorities dithered and worried about the wisdom of such behaviour, and while they procrastinated Mother Earth took matters into her own hands, as parts of Cleator Moor started to sink in to the mines taking houses and a school with it.

The enterprises around Moor Row involved a handful of people getting dizzyingly rich, and the thousands of families who did the heavy work. The iron and steel industry of the area lasted about eighty years before it expired, leaving a legacy of transplanted families. Some people left the area looking for work. The majority remained and watched the railways close and the steel furnaces extinguished, waiting for a change in fortunes. From 1924 to 1937, seven thousand people were sacked from the sixteen thousand who worked in the Cumbrian iron making and mining businesses, as three thousand new jobs were taken up in hotels, building and delivery work[2]. As extractive industries like mining and quarrying declined, so too did manufacturing until in the 2020s the main work of the area was service based.[3]

---

[2] Daysh, G H J, 1938: p117-118.
[3] A service is something made and used at the same time, like eating at a restaurant, visiting the dentist, cleaning, using a bank account or painting a house. Goods are things that are portable and durable like cars, clothes, guns, houses, and tins of paint.

CHAPTER 2

BRITAIN'S HISTORY IN MOOR ROW

There is a story in Barrow in Furness that England is an island off the east coast of Walney. Similarly, it often appears that Britain is a valley past the hills that protect Lamplugh from the easterly wind. Although the main interest of this essay is Moor Row a short account of the growth of being English before 1891 will show some of the concerns the ruling classes interested themselves in.

Written records of the area become accessible from about the year 1100, when the invading Normans from France started to organise their new territories after the last ever English King Harold Godwin was killed in the battle at Hastings.[4] By organise, we mean to measure farm sizes, and farm out puts, and then to keep written records of the wealth in the country to raise taxes for the royal rulers. This close scrutiny started to bring the country in to a single ruling court of people living mainly in the expanding city of London. Having a single city and royal family in charge meant rules about succession were made, and rules about how to behave and keep the peace were developed so money was not wasted in petty wars when disputes broke out. Having rules also meant trade could be controlled and the wealth and power of a country increased- called mercantilism.

There have been 43 monarchs since King Harold died in battle at Hastings.

---

[4] Harold was also the last elected King of Britain, selected by the leading landowners of the country after King Edward the Confessor had died.

The King and Queen monarchs have come from Scottish, Welsh, Spanish and German families. Only one, Richard II died in battle, while four were murdered and one was executed. At least nineteen died of serious disease. There was also one period when no King ruled at all, when Oliver Cromwell presided over a republic in the 1600s supported by the army.[5]

The youngest monarchs were Henry VI who took over the throne when six months old, and Mary Queen of Scots who was six days old when she ascended the Scottish throne. Charles III is the oldest to ascend the throne, at seventy-three years.

The families of monarchs tend to have their names used to described periods in Britain's growth, hence Tudor, Stuart, Victorian and Edwardian periods. Royal periods are used to describe the improvements that are derived from living within in a British cult, without actually saying what being British might mean, or which particular people are being described.

After the Normans and Plantagenets, the warring cousins from Lancaster and York fought themselves to a marriage deal to form the Welsh royal clan of Tudor. The Welsh Tudor family continued the integration of England in to a London bureaucracy which helped to support the cult of a divinely appointed monarch. The Tudors closed the monasteries and used their stone walls as quarries to build new town houses and manors as the new class of landed gentry usurped the power of feudal nobility. These new middle class salesmen used the wealth from commerce to buy position, power and favour in the royal court at London and promote themselves through sponsoring the cult of Elizabethan monarchy which had apparently calmed the disputes along the Scots border, fostering a more settled existence that brought the sense of propriety through life lived in one place and treated mobile workers with deep suspicion. The Tudor century between the years 1500 and 1600 also brought harvest failures and famine, as well as plague

---

[5] Richard II, Edward V, William II, Edward II, were murdered, Charles I was executed, and Oliver Cromwell died of malaria. Serious diseases that were fatal for British monarchs were cancer, tuberculosis, obesity, leprosy, food poisoning, dysentery, pox, heart disease, pyphoria, and stroke.

and wars. Eventually the Tudors ran out of male heirs and handed the crown to the Stuart clan of Scotland.

The Stuart century of 1600 to 1700 saw the kingdom of England and Scotland combined together. The period is famous for the war between the Kings army and the Parliament army which got a king executed. The failed attempts to kill the first Stuart King gave us bonfire parties on Guy Fawkes night. The King gave his people a new version of the Bible and a book on how to kill witches. Later the Great Fire of London, caused by a bakers shop catching fire, led to new laws about how to build houses using stone. The Stuarts invented coffee shops, bananas, dining forks, colonies in North America for white men, scientific experiments, typhoid and sewers. The nobility ran out of good ideas for a new Scottish King and had to pick a German who was fifty second in line to the throne from Hanover and could not speak English. They liked to be called George, and Britain had four kings with that name, one of which gave the colonies away to the white colonial men in America, and then a King William and a Queen called Victoria. Victoria was a German and married a German Prince called Albert Sax Coburg Gotha.

It was Queen Victoria who ruled Britain when Moor Row was first being built and during her long reign the country became disciplined, organised and regulated so that everyone knew their place and knew what they had to do in their life. Life for working people treated them as parts of a great steam powered machine that needed people to turn up and do as they were told, without complaint or failure under threat of being thrown in to jail or the workhouse or deported to prisons in Australia. This needed a sense of involvement and improvement to be forced on people, so the Victorians invented street lights to keep the shops open longer, a police force to round up trouble makers, health boards, schools for children under ten years old to get them ready for work, and societies and clubs. The societies and clubs were for reading groups, to restrain from drinking of alcohol, military drill halls, Christian worship and bible study, organising town life and punishing unwanted behaviour, standardising education to government plans, spreading news by newspapers and books, and political clubs to encourage aggressive nationalist campaigns. The standardisation to London rules was said to bring democracy to the working people of the country, but it did not improve working conditions, the standard of housing or health care. Nor did democracy reduce the extent or effects of malnutrition. The improvements of the age brought us the Football Association and the Rugby Football Union and their rules on how grown ups must compete in a game played in the street by free spirited children.

Queen Victoria's grandson, King George V changed the family name to Windsor in 1917 when a German Gotha G.IV aeroplane dropped bombs on London after Britain had declared war against Germany in 1914. The war consumed all of Europe and killed about 40 million people.

A calendar of how Britain figured in Moor Row's history shows how important the village has been to the country.

1100s Norman castles are built in Cockermouth and Egremont, followed by the establishment of market places.

1179 William 3rd Earl of Albemarle gives his iron mine at Egremont to the Abbey of Holme Cultram.

1300s Whitehaven is a small village for fisherman. The main businesses are milling, weaving, lime quarrying and leather tanning in the Egremont, Cleator, Cockermouth area.

1350 Cockermouth and Egremont are attacked by Scots soldiers led by Robert the Bruce.

1364 French language replaced by English as the national language of England.

1565 South Bridge Egremont built in stone as part of the towns improvements along the main street and in the marketplace.

1615 Scalegill Hall Moor Row built.

1630 Whitehaven stone pier built to load coal on to ships for Ireland.

1660 Stone buildings start to replace wooden houses along Egremont main street.

1670 William Coates rents his land to Thomas Patrickson of Castle How Ennerdale to mine for iron.

1682 William and John Coates rent their land at Woodend to Thomas Addison of Whitehaven to mine for iron.

1694 Charcoal fuelled blast furnace built at Cleator.

1728 Frizington blast furnace being tested.

1743 Whitehaven Workhouse for paupers opened at Scotch Street to join the Preston Quarter work house. The building was replaced in 1854 with the new built Union Workhouse for 420 'pauper inmates' next to the cemetery on the St Bees road. Renamed a Public Assistance Institution in 1930, and then became a geriatric hospital. The Union Workhouse building was demolished in 1960s as it was collapsing in to mine workings.

1750 Briscoe Bridge built below Cobra Castle by the Egremont hat maker John Pearson.

1750s Whitehaven trade grows to include shipping tobacco, rum, sugar and limes through the harbour.

1753 Crowgarth iron ore being mined by Peter Howe, Will Hicks and G Griffiths, Whitehaven traders of Virginia tobacco.

1768 Thomas Dalzell, also spelt as Dalziel, married Elizabeth Wildrige of Moor Row at St James Church in Whitehaven. Elizabeth was daughter of John Wildridge and his wife Elizabeth, who owned bits of land around Moor Row.

1772 Crowgarth ore mined by James Spedding.

1782 Wath forge rented from Daniel Baynes by Thomas Dixon and Reverend Colquhoun.

1788 William Walker opens a coal mine in Cleator Moor.

1792 Crowgarth mine leased to John Litt and the Cleator bacon maker Jonas Lindow.

1797 Jacktrees mine opened.

1783 Whitehaven Medical Dispensary opened by James Hogarth at 107 Queen Street Whitehaven, replaced in 1830 with Howgill Infirmary. Whitehaven Castle hospital opened 1924. Hensingham hospital opened 1964 and renovated in 2021. There was a fever hospital in The Ginns area after 1819 for controlling the spread of typhus fever, and a small pox hospital at Bransty.

1784 Crowgarth mine working an 8 metre band of iron ore at a depth of 4 metres, sending 20,000 tons a year in 1790 to the Carron Foundry in Scotland.

1787 John Collier killed by roof fall in Threapthwaite colliery at Bowthorn.

1790 The Dalzell map of the Moor Row area shows just one farm building, a water well, and the routes of three roads from the 1500s which became Dalzell Street, Scalegill Road and Church Street.

1800 Henry Birley builds Cleator flax mill on site of old iron furnace. The Birley family were merchants of Kirkham Lancashire and Egremont.

1815 Battle of Waterloo, the end of the Napoleonic War.

1815 Threapthwaite mine, worked by John Litt and Company for sale.

1815 Seven million square metres of common land fenced in across Cleator Moor and Dent and shared out as land enclosures start.

1822 Cleator forge owners Little, Lindow and Allinson take over the Wath forge.

1825 Crowgarth mine leased to Anthony Hill

1826 John McGinnis killed in Mr Fresh's Langhorn iron pit at Egremont, leaving six young children unprovided for..

1829 Anthony Dalzell leases land to Anthony Hill to mine for iron ore at Moor Row.

1831 Whitehaven has its first street lights, lit by gas.

1837 Carlisle to Gateshead railway opened.

1839 Thomas Christian killed at the Lindow mine at Woodend.

1840 Cleator Moor mine raising ore for Ainsworths Whitehaven Iron Company.

1843 First iron produced at Cleator Moor furnaces.

1845 Thomas Tubman dies at work in Attwoods Frizington iron mine.

1846 Gutterby mine opened.

1846 Lancaster Carlisle railway line opened.

1848 Forty two thousand potters counted passing through Bassenthwaite looking for work.

1853 Ainsworth's Cleator Moor Mining Company break in to the Crossfield mine area, leased by Anthony Hill, to improve access to their own ore.

1855 The Whitehaven Cleator and Egremont Railway (WC&ER) comes to Moor Row from Whitehaven.

1856 Six people in Bowthorn Road killed by poison gas from furnace waste while they were in bed.

1856 The WC&ER Moor Row to Egremont extension line is opened.

1857 Railway through connection from Carlisle to Whitehaven to Lancaster is opened.

1858 The Moor Row to Egremont railway line damaged by collapsing in to mine workings, requiring a new viaduct and replacement embankments near Woodend.

1858 The first Cleator Moor Co-Operative store opened.

1860 Ingwell Mansion, Low Hall and Galemire estates at Moor Row bought by John Lindow of Croft End, Woodend.

1860 Crossfield mine opened.

1862 Montreal mine opened by John Stirling.

1863 Primitive Wesleyan chapel opened in Scalegill Road Moor Row, which closed in 1878.

1865 Cleator Moor residents buying their drinking water from the Montreal mines.

1865 Crowgarth mine being worked by Lord Leconfield the land owner.

1866 Cleator Moor railway station moved after sinking in to mine workings.

1867 Jacktrees mine hospital opened in Cleator Moor.

1869 Lord Lowther and Lord Leconfield each making the equivalent of £8.5 million a year from their Cumbrian businesses.

1869 Cleator Moor water works built on Dent.

1870 Ben Mitchell of Moor Row crushed in Moor Row mine.

1872 Parton iron works opened. Closed down 1883.

1872 Lonsdale iron works opened at Bransty. Closed in 1896. Knocked down 1904.

1872 Miners Association formed for West Cumberland coal miners.

1872 Ainsworth Cleator Moor Mining Company sued for improperly removing 10,000 tons of ore from the Crossfield Company mining area[6].

---

[6] *Whitehaven News* 1/ 2/ 1872 'Important Local Mining Case'.

1873 Thirty nine blast furnaces working in Cumberland.

1875 United Methodist Free Church chapel built in Scalegill Road, Moor Row. Closed and merged with School Street in 1961.

1874 Cleator Moor gas works opens on Birks Road, supplying Cleator, Woodend, Gutterby, Moor Row, and Scalegill Place.

1877 Cleator Moor gas street lights being installed.

1878 Cleator Moor fire brigade started.

1878 Moor Row Church Street Primitive Wesleyan chapel opened. Closed in 1940.

1879 Galemire Fever Hospital opened.

1879 Cleator Moor market hall built on land used to keep pigs on. In 1966 it burned down.

1879 Longlands mine opened.

1879 Fawn Cross farm house and buildings sink completely in to mine workings. The original Fallen Cross way side marker was recovered and put in the gardens of Flosh mansion.

1880 St John the Evangelist church opened.

1880 Moor Row school opened.

1880 Miners strike to reduce working days to less than fourteen hours.

1881 Peak iron ore extraction reached in Cumberland, of 1,600,000 tons in the year. Such a weight of haematite having specific gravity of 5 would form a cube with sides of 68 metres.

1885 Row Foot mine opened.

1886 Wesleyan chapel and school built in School Street. Closed 1969.

1889 Postlethwaite mines at Moor Row prosecuted for running a dangerous mine.

1891 Electric street lights installed at Whitehaven.

1891 Workers Association formed for West Cumberland Iron Ore miners.

1893 First domestic electric supply in Whitehaven supplied from the engine house at the sewage pumping works on West Strand.

1897 United Methodist Free Church school built in Scalegill Road. Closed and merged with School Street in 1961.

1898 The first motor car to be seen in Penrith is reported in the local newspaper.

1899 Britain sends soldiers to South Africa to fight the Boers.

1901 Whitehaven Harriers stop fox hunting around West Cumberland (now called Cumbria).

1904 Andrew Carnegie of America opens the first of four public libraries in the old Cumberland, at Workington, Whitehaven, Cleator Moor, and Cockermouth as part of his plan to donate his one billion pound fortune to charitable work. In 2022 that one billion would be worth a £152 billion give away.

1904 Lonsdale Iron Works at Bransty demolished.

1909 Eight Penzance Street building plots sold by the Dalzell estate to the Moor Row builder Athanasius Chapple, for £204 the lot.

1913 Fire in William Stirlings number 3 mine, Cleator Moor closes down three other mines from smoke. Whitehaven Colliery Rescue Brigade, Cleator Moor fire brigade and Whitehaven brigade in attendance. Leconfield's Crowgarth Mine, Crossfield Co's No. 1, and Stirling's No. 6 and No. 4 all affected through underground tunnels.

1914 Britain declares war on Germany in August.

1920 Moor Row war memorial built.

1922 Second Labour MP for Whitehaven elected. Thomas Gavan Duffy had his offices in Moor Row.

1922 Egremont council rent land from Dalzell estates for £16 per year, to sub let as allotments in Moor Row.

1924 Cleator Moor electricity power station opens.

1933 Kelton Fell railway closed.

1935 Public passenger train services stopped at Moor Row.

1938 Kangol hat factory opened at Cleator mills, closed 2009.

1939 Last Moor Row mine abandoned and left to flood.

1939 Britain declares war on Germany in September.

1941 Explosive and propellant factories built at Sellafield and Drigg.

1946 Montreal School Cleator Moor and its 30 metre high clock tower closed and demolished as surrounding streets start collapsing in to mine workings.

1948 Ingwell Mansion at Moor Row, and land, sold to Cumbria Council.

1948 Crowgarth pit in Cleator Moor is closed

1950 Sellafield's Windscale factory starts making plutonium for nuclear bombs.

1950 Rowntree build a chocolate factory near Christie Bridge, Egremont, replaced with York Place houses in 2005.

1951 60,000 British soldiers sent to fight in Korean war.

1953 Queen Elizabeth 2nd's coronation celebration party in Moor Row village hall in Penzance Street.

1953 Velda Cook born, cousin of Bob Maxwell who was killed in Postlethwaites mine in Moor Row.

1954 Horses used on farms in America become out numbered by tractors on farms.

1956 Britain sends soldiers to Suez to fight Egyptian troops.

1957 Sellafield first plutonium factory closed after it caught fire. All milk for 200 miles around was poured down drains because it was dangerous, and 90 tons of chocolate made at the Rowntree factory at Egremont was thrown away. Plutonium for weapons was made at Calder Hall and Chapelcross reactors instead.

1960s Station Terrace Moor Row, Scalegill Place terraces and Gutterby houses demolished.

1961 First manned space flight by Yuri Gagarin of Russia.

1961 Kristina Cook born, cousin of Bob Maxwell who was killed in Postlethwaite's mine in Moor Row.

1964 Wyndham School Egremont opened, rebuilt as West Lakes Academy 2012, sponsored by nuclear waste companies.

1965 Workmens train service from Moor Row to Sellafield stopped.

1969 First manned landing on the moon, Neil Armstrong and Edwin Buzz Aldrin of USA.

1971 Britain stops using money in Pounds Shillings and Pence (£ s d) and uses Pounds and decimal Pence instead (£ P).

1974 County of Cumbria created from Cumberland, Westmorland, parts of Yorkshire and parts of Lancashire.

1974 Moss Bay Workington steel works closed, the last one in West Cumbria

1980 Mineral trains from Beckermet mine through Moor Row stopped, and the line through Moor Row completely closed..

1980 Beckermet mine, last working ore mine in Cumbria, closed.

1981 The 262 acre estate of Ingwell Mansion is taken over as Westlakes Science Park of 130 acres. That's a square of land of 1000 metres each side reduced to a square of 752 metres each side.

1982 The Spedding house of Summergrove Mansion, Moor Row, knocked down for Sellafield worker hostel Summergrove Hall.

1990s Pearson Close, Moor Row, built.

1993 All railway track lifted from Moor Row and sold for scrap metal.

1994 Path from Whitehaven to Rowrah opened through Moor Row along the old railway line, part of the C2C route that goes to Sunderland.

1997 Sophie Cook born, cousin of Bob Maxwell who was killed in Postlethwaites mine in Moor Row.

2000 The first crew to live on board the International Space Station arrive in orbit using a Russian Soyuz space craft launched from Baikonur in Kazakhstan.

2004 Larch Court, Moor Row, houses being built.

2005 Houses at Greenmoor Road, Egremont, are evacuated as gardens sink in to old mines. The had to be knocked down because they could not be repaired.

2009 Harley Reece Young born.

2007 Florence Mine left to flood when drain pumps turned off.

2012 Eight houses in Howbank Road Egremont evacuated as gardens sink in to old mines.

2013 Lexi May Willan born.

2016 Sienna Charlotte Young born.

2018 Harry Cook born in Londonderry, cousin of Bob Maxwell who was killed in Postlethwaites mine in Moor Row.

2020 Thomas Lucre Young born.

2020 COVID 19 epidemic breaks out world wide. UK government orders closure of schools, shops, businesses, cafés, cinemas in Britain and people told to stay in doors and not to be within 2 metres of some one else. The first restrictions lasted 13 weeks, from March 23rd to June 23rd, and 52,000 people died in that period, the highest in Europe at the time. By Christmas 2022 there had been 212,000 deaths and 24 million confirmed cases in Britain.

2020 Sienna Young spent the summer playing with sand pits and trucks, tennis and ten pin bowling, making Play-doh meals, painting faces, having tea parties with Velda, watering the plants, topping up the bird feeders, going lamping in the dark, and feeding the pet stone cats at Moor Row station.

2020 Rusper Drive, Moor Row, houses being built.

2022 Sellafield stops treating used nuclear fuel.

2022 Charles, Prince of Wales, becomes King Charles III and inherits control of the monarchs land, palaces, castles, jewels, and paintings worth £40 billion, without any tax to be paid, plus a further £500 million of personal belongings, also without any tax to be paid.

2022 The UK Government offer hospital nurses a pay rise of £1400 a year which will take the average pay of a nurse to £35000 in a year. Every nurse will payback £8000 a year in taxes to the UK government.

Chapter 3

NORMANS, MONKS, CATTLE THIEVES AND ACCOUNTANTS.

A long time ago Moor Row was nothing more than the point were the roads between Egremont, Hensingham, St Bees and Frizington all crossed.

The land was rough pasture[7] and the houses were homesteads for people that lived off the land. The roads were earth tracks across fields running between hedges. The living was made by growing vegetables through spring and summer, fattening animals in summer and autumn, and spreading manure in winter to help the vegetables and grass grow for the next spring.

The residents got their water in buckets from rivers, springs or wells, and spread their muck on the fields around their houses.

The places the people lived in the 1700s along the boundary between the fields and the common land, at Cleator Moor and on Dent fell sides.

Houses at Todholes, Crowgarth, Aldby, Black How, Roe Foot, Cobra Castle and Cote Close were built in the 1600s for easy access to cultivated

---

[7] Hutchinson wrote in 1797 the soil was largely clay, cold and wet around Cleator, growing mainly barley and oats. The farmers, he said, did not work hard, growing just a few potatoes but no turnips, and no fallow land made up. The houses were good, the people were rich, and the roads were bad, (p29). Distington lands are described as cold, wet and barren, much neglected by the farmers who mainly worked as carters to the ports, (p99); Lamplugh harvests were late due to coldness (p97); Ennerdale is melancholy, (p137) [W. Hutchinson, *The History of the County of Cumberland* 1797, reprinted EP Publishing Wakefield, 1974.

land and common grazing[8]. The area had been organised by Norman Barons who arrived after the 1066 battle at Hastings, and administered by Norman churches until Henry VIII closed them down in the 1500s. King Henry handed the church lands to the aristocracy of Barons and left some open for grazing. The open grazing land was called 'common land' or 'commons'[9] hence the name 'commoners' for people who used such land.

Until the 1600s Cumberland was preyed upon by Scots reivers[10], just as Cumbrian raiders rampaged around Dumfries. When the Scots King James VI became King of England there was a stop put to all the nonsense in the interests of a new nation of Britain. In the 1650s Britain survived without a King when Cromwell and Parliament ran the country and the Cumbria landowners did their best to stay out of the fighting to preserve their fortunes. In 1745 the Scots Bonnie Prince Charlie[11] marched south through Cumberland to Manchester and Derby, to claim his British throne. A few weeks later he retreated to Culloden in Scotland, and then left for Italy.

In the 1800s the industrialist invaded with mills, machines, railways and ambitions to improve their lot by digging up everything of value under the ground and selling it. Around 1815 the open commons of Dent and

---

[8] At Cote Close the stables have a date stone marked '1629' on the stable wall above the horse mount, facing the yard gate. Bowthorn had a date stone marked E S M 1685. Crossfield, the old home of the Benn family, had a door lintel dated 1688 to the back of the house. Black How home stead has a date stone bearing the marks ILA 1762. The stone was brought by Jonas and Agnes Lindow from their former home on Cleator main street. They bought Black How from the Benn family in 1846, the Benns having lived there since 1576 when an early family member of Black How, John Benn, is known to have died there.

[9] The Egremont alley way 'Common Gate' at No 15 Main St. formed the entrance to a path leading to common land and a common well, at the back of Lowes Court (itself built in the 1600s). The path also gave access to 'Rose Cottage', replaced by the Wyndham Mine buildings in the 1880s.

[10] Reivers - Gangs of sheep and cow thieves.

[11] Bonnie Prince Charlie, heir to the throne of Great Britain, was of Polish and German ancestry, and Grandson of King James II of Britain. Monarchies do use weird methods to get the preferred person to be king or queen.

Cleator, around seven million square metres were fenced off and given or sold to local homesteaders:[12] That's the same size as 3700 football pitches. The expectation was private ownership would encourage improvement of the land which would be made more productive.[13]

The local families that got the larger plots were those of Troughton, Fisher, Hartley, Braddyll[14], Mossop, Tyson, Towersons, Birley, Little, Lindow, Gaitskell, Nicholson, Shephard (119 acres), The Reverend Dalziel, Sir Alan Chambers, The Earl of Egremont, Mr John Dalziel, The Reverend John Benson, and Mr Joseph Benn (87 acres). The largest area of one million square metres (291 acres) was bought by Humphrey Senhouse.

The largest plots given away for free went to Joseph Benn who got 49 acres, the Earl of Egremont (49 acres), T R G Braddyll (349 acres), John, Jane and Henry Birley (19, 8 and 13 acres each), and the Reverend Benson, who was given 26 acres-illustrating the church teachings of how some of the meek will inherit the earth in preparation for inheriting the kingdom of God.

Along the Cumberland coast other landowners had already built up large plots of land, like the Lowther family, led by the Earl of Lonsdale. Lowthers owned land from Bootle near Millom, up through Egremont and out to the Workington and Lamplugh regions. Comparing the development of different parishes from 1801 shows how large industries that are well connected to customers, can drastically alter the character of an area. Consider Bootle, Arlecdon and Cleator, each of about 350 residents in 1801, living on land part owned by Lowther, each of about 3000 to 5000 acres of rough land, growing the same crops, living in similar houses.

---

[12] Caine (1916) pp165- 170.

[13] In the 1800s the land area was measured using imperial units not metric, called acres. Each acre being the same as about 4000 square metres, that could be enclosed by a square of 63 metres sides. 'Acre' is the old word for 'field', being the area that could be ploughed in a day by a pair of oxen. A football pitch is about one and three quarters acres.

[14] Col. Thomas Richmond Gale Bradyll of Conishead Priory Ulverston, obtained his acres by right of tithes. His family comes from Catgill Hall Egremont, Bardsea Hall Urswick, and Highhead Castle near Carlisle. He went bankrupt through mining investments in Durham coal mines. There is a pub named after the family in Ulverston.

Arlecdon grew in 100 hundred years to have a railway, iron ore mines at Frizington, an 80 metre deep colliery at Asby, quarries, and 6000 people living in terraced cottages. The work brought 3 schools, 47 shops, a library and council offices, a fire station, a police sergeant, a piped water supply, and oil powered street lighting. There were four social clubs, for Liberals, Conservatives, Working Men and the Saint Josephs club, and a branch of the Pearl Assurance company. As the towns grew the streets started to be named after local business men. Frizington got a street named after the Lindow family.

Cleator and Cleator Moor showed the same cosmopolitan developments. They had streets named after Wyndhams and Leconfields and the Stirling accident hospital named after an owner of local mines.[15] In 100 years the population had grown to ten thousand people, with four schools for two thousand children. The town had grown enough to bury the remains of the Roman road that passed through Cleator. It had a gas works, iron ore mines, a flax mill, a pig iron factory, a brewery, 280 shops, football club, workers association, a resident professor of music and had created the unusual job of a 'river watcher' who lived at Dent Cottage on the fell side.

Bootle in 1901 had continued its rural manners of a former market town. The population rose to about 800 in 100 years. A gun range for Vickers ship builders had opened in the sand dunes at Eskmeals and a Work House built. There were 15 shops, 5 tradesmen selling seeds, corn and such like, two schools, an Oddfellows lodge, 2 banks, 3 hostelries, one police constable and a resident artillery gunner. Bootle range was built on Lowther land, but the town had not developed any of the cosmopolitan amenities seen at Arlecdon or Cleator. The high technology work at the new gun range, and the skilled workers required to staff it did not compensate at all for the lack of iron and of being a market town in decline. Moor Row, in contrast, had swollen by having managers, business proprietors, and professional workers in the town that also housed the hewers, diggers and muscle to do the work in the mines and the skilled men required to operate a railway.

---

[15] The matron is recorded as Mrs Corkhill [Bulmers 1901, p535], but no staff are listed.

It had become a Cleator Moor in miniature, and Cleator Moor resembled West Cumberland in miniature. The residents had been shipped in to West Cumberland to be groomed to dig iron ore from underground, convert it to high value iron and steel, and hand over the profits to the business owners in return for tough times living hand to mouth under constant threat of being a destitute in the Work House or mutilated at work.

There were two public houses in Moor Row, a school for five hundred and thirty boys, girls and infants, a reading room, working men's institute, two insurance agencies, and a wine and spirits store. The Rev Wharton had moved in. The nearest fire stations were at Lamb Lane and Bookwell in Egremont and Quarry Road in Cleator Moor. An isolation hospital for twenty contagious patients had been built in two buildings at Galemire on the road to Keekle.

Bulmer listed some residents of Moor Row in 1901.

Chapple and Sons the builders lived at 36 Church Street and ran an agency for the Royal Fife and Life insurance company.

Henry Hartley of Moor Row Farm worked as an agent for the Ocean Accident and Guarantee Insurance company.

Joseph Dalzell ran the wine and spirit store.

Henry Doloughan of 26 Scalegill Road was proprietor of a quarry.

William Postlethwaite the railway traffic controller, lived at Alva House.

Edwin Rose was an engineer who lived in Victoria Villa.

John Asking was a draper at 49 Dalzell Street, John Webb sold clogs from 48 Dalzell Street, William Brown at 51 was a grocers. John Mossop was also a grocer at number 7.

George White sold shoes from 69 Penzance Street.

William Horne worked from 32 Church Street as a hairdresser.

Wilson Michelson was a tailor, and **William Steele** the postmaster.

Moor Row, despite its small size, showed a diversity of residents, from theological students, business proprietors, professional workers, to the clerical staff, trades workers and skilled labourers who made the money while taking the risks. The village also adopted the new obsequious practice of naming streets after local landowners for the workers to be reminded of their great and good on their way to work. The suburban gentility of parts of the village were set apart and enhanced by detached houses using distinctive names rather than numbers, a practice that was continued in the 1980s along the Gutterby road using names for modern houses. The names Dalzell, John, Pearson, Hollins, Montreal and William distinguish streets and serve as a reminder of who really owned the land the town is built on.

Chapter 4

MOOR ROW WAS ONCE A MOOR

In 1800 Moor Row did not exist as a village.[16] The land between Bigrigg and Cleator was poor ground, fit mainly for cows and sheep to forage for grass and to recycle dung on. There was none of the soil management that distinguishes land for growing crops on.

The local residents lived on homesteads where they grew vegetables and fattened their animals for their own food, selling what was left over for cash to buy whatever else they needed and couldn't make themselves.

Around Woodend and Keekle the homesteaders grew barley, oats, turnips, and grass in sodden clay soil. Very few people lived in the area until the 1850s.[17]

Government records of 1841 listed residents around Moor Row as:

Woodend: Samuel Lindow, 60 years old, (industrialist),[18] and

---

[16] Named as Low Keekle shown on the 1863 Ordnance Survey Map, National Library of Scotland Map Images. www.maps.nls.uk/view/102340887

[17] Between 1801 to 1841 only St. Bees with Whitehaven saw a large increase in Population, from 13,000 to 20,000. Other parishes grew much more slowly: Arlecdon, shrunk from 366 to 211. Cleator grew from 362 to 763. Bootle 547 to 800. Egremont 1500 to 1750. Workington stayed about the same at 7000 [Mannix and Whelan 1847, p309].

[18] The Lindow family came from the Furness area of Lancashire, and had fingers in many pies, from pork butchery and bacon curing, landownership, spade making, mining, railways.. The bacon factory was at Kiln Brow, in Cleator on the right hand side of the road descending to the river.

agriculturalist with 4 servants. Also, John Birley, 70, an industrialist,[19] Ann Jackson, aged 60 lived alone at Croft End on her own means. Woodend Mill was occupied by John Turner, living with six more people.

Gutterby Gate: Alexander Knight, aged 55, an agricultural labourer.

Moor Row: Thirty two people lived in the area that became Moor Row: Anthony Iredale, aged 35, living with two others; James Steele, aged 20, a tile moulder living with four others. John Iredale, aged 30, Homesteader, living with four people; James Russell, aged 30 living with six others; John Hitton, aged 60 a homesteader living with nine others; William Tyson, aged 70 living with one other.

Shaw: Hannah Usher, aged 60, homesteader living with five others.

At Bigrigg, Springfield, and Park House there were six more households of 25 people in total, headed by labourers, homesteaders, and a washer woman.

Bigrigg Moor had six households with 36 residents working as labourers, masons, house wrights, and black smiths.

Orepit House had four households of 25 people- carpenters, masons, labourers and a blacksmith.

Summerhill was worked by John Fisher, aged 47, with 12 other people. Kell Head was occupied by John Benn, aged 57, described as a yeoman. Snellings was occupied by Anthony Dixon, aged 22 and described as a 'gentleman' with 10 more people. John Towerson aged 66, and 3 more people also lived at Snelllings. Thomas Hartley, aged 38, a merchant, lived with 10 others at Gillfoot.

Blackling, Catgill, Picklhall, Catgill Hall, and Green Dykes were occupied by homesteaders.

---

[19] Birley owned the Cleator flax mill that went bankrupt. The mill was built on the site of an iron furnace, that had gone bankrupt. Birley sold his mill and house to Ainsworth, a member of a Preston family who ran many mills in Lancashire that went bankrupt. Whenever a business went bankrupt workers lost their jobs and their health and security was put in jeapordy.

Many of these had benefited by allotments granted to them by enclosure of common land in the area and they set about finding ways to increase the money made from their land. Although some small homesteads survived enclosures and carried on working until the 1900s, many were lost or sold out. Many residents also failed to preserve their claim to minerals under the ground they lived on, or sold them without realising their value.

By 1851 in Moor Row, John Hitton and John Iredale were working about 130 acres with seven servants each. Isaac Dalzell of Lamplugh had set up as a butcher, with four more people in his household plus his son John S Dalzell aged 9. Around Moor Row a greater variety of work had developed. At Bigrigg, Gutterby, Woodend, Rose Castle and Shaw there were also iron miners, engine operators, locomotive drivers, ore salesmen, grooms, engineers, masons, corn millers, flax spinners, cordwainers, and carpenters. The homesteaders were making a bit more on the side, like John Spedding, who described himself as a miller and a farmer. There was even the civilising influence of William Leech, the Rector[20] of Egremont living at Rose Castle Rectory with 12 more in the household and three servants, meekly waiting to inherit the earth, but not its mineral rights.

In 1891 the fifth decennal government census was taken for the whole of Britain. The census showed that many of the 228 'Heads of Household' in Moor Row and Scalegill were 'off-comers', that is, born outside Cumberland. In fact 115 of the 228 were off-comers: one each from Wales and Italy; 9 from Ireland; 3 from Isle of Man; 17 from Scotland; 51 from Cornwall, and 33 from the other English counties outside Cumberland. Two notable points can also be seen in the 1891 census which are worthy of comment,

- There are very few empty houses in Moor Row and Scalegill, and
- There are no unemployed heads of households.

This might be explained by the recurring 10 year cycle of output for British heavy industry and a corresponding employment cycle [Boyer 2002]. The census year 1891 was a high point for employment, with unemployment

---

[20] Rector is a senior vicar.

peaks five years before and after the census. Secondly, the work house roll was higher than the previous years in 1891 and wages were reported as depressed in newspaper reports, forced down by owners competing on low prices for iron. Unfortunately unions did not commonly pay unemployment support until later in the 1890s so miners would be forced to take pay cuts to keep the family in a house.

In 1891 the biggest employer for Moor Row and Scalegill residents was the ore mines, employing 170 men. The railway employed 154 men. Women were employed in domestic service (12), dress making (27) and teaching (4 of the 7 teachers resident in Moor Row were women). Twenty woman residents were recorded as agricultural workers on homesteads, otherwise they were described as 'wife', 'daughter', or 'scholar'. Twenty five people lived off their own means, meaning they were widowed, retired, or taking in boarders. There were 30 skilled tradesmen, like smiths, joiners, painters, a mason and a miller. There were 53 people providing services, like 8 grocers, 7 teachers and a school caretaker, 17 clerical staff, 4 shoe sellers or makers, a clock maker, 4 mineral borers, 3 tailors, a carter, a lodging house proprietor, three inn keepers, a theological student, a coal merchant, and a sewing machine agent.

Ninety years on, in 1980 the main businesses had closed. The mines had become muddy lakes or mounds of left over muck. The railway was stripped in 1995 and sold as scrap metal leaving a cinder track running 7 miles between Whitehaven and Rowrah. Eventually it was covered in tarmacadam and turned in to a footpath and cycle way forming 7 miles of the 137 miles route crossing England to Sunderland. The trees growing along the cycle path in 2022 have all grown since the railway closed, crowding the few platforms left along the path at Moor Row, Parkside and Frizington for instance. In the years between 1891 to 1980 the village of Moor Row had been compared to the national railway network centre based at Crewe. In 2022 it was on a junction of two routes of a national cycle network, run by a charity based in Bristol. While the railway thrived, it fed the steel making industries of Cumberland, Wales and Scotland in an industrial boom likened to the Klondike gold rush. Fortunes were made.

Moor Row in 1891

By 2022 Moor Row had grown from about ten houses in 1800 to 500 houses, in Dalzell Street, Penzance Street, Church Street, John Street, Scalegill Road, Pearson Close, Montreal Place, Hollins Park, West Spur, Larch Court, Scalegill Place and School Street. More houses were being built in Rusper Drive as well. The village in 2022 had turned in to a dormitory settlement;[21] a place for people to go home to after work or school for a meal and a sleep. The businesses in the village were two car repair garages, a working men's club, and a nail bar.

Back in 1891 the notable buildings mentioned in the census are:

Church Street: Number (No.) 1, a Grocers, No 3 a licensed bar, No 4 a Spirit Vaults, No 5 a Co-Operative store, No 8 a Drapers, No 28 was joined to No 1 Scalegill Road. No 32 a Reading Room. Also a Primitive Methodist Chapel and Sunday School.

Dalzell Street: No. 1 the Station Hotel, and a Grocers shop at No 7 and a Shoe & Boot shop at No 48. The Working Men's Institute was not mentioned.

Scalegill: Nos 1 & 2 was the Beehive public house, No 17 was a lodging house, No. 20 a Grocers, and No 60 the Bay Horse Inn.

Scalegill Road: No. 14 Grocers shop. The United Methodist Free Chapel and Sunday School.

School Street: the Moor Row Board School, and Wesleyan Chapel with Sunday School.

Station Terrace: the Moor Row Junction railway station.

In 1891 there were five iron ore mines working around Moor Row, called Crossfield, Montreal, Moor Row, Fletcher and MossBay.

---

[21] A dormitory settlement increases in size due to residents moving in from nearby urban areas. Incomers retain jobs in the urban area to which they commute, leading to decline in village services as they prefer to spend most of their money outside the settlement, travelling to shops in private transport.

Chapter 5

MOOR ROW RESIDENTS 1891
Organised by Streets.

Church Street Moor Row in 1891

1 Church St., was a grocers shop occupied by 4 people: William Steele, 42, from Drigg, the grocer and shop keeper; wife Ann, 37; and daughters Jane, 3 and Margaret, 9 years old.

2 Church St., was occupied by 4 people: Samuel Wills, widow, 43, from St. Dennis, Cornwall; two sons John and Charles; and his niece Fanny Wills, 19, of St. Dennis who worked as a housekeeper.

3 Church St., a licensed Beer House, occupied by 3 people: James Binning, 67 a mineral borer from Scotland and Beer House Keeper; wife Jane, 62; and Laura, grand daughter, 10. Laura's mother, another Jane, was also registered at the house in 1901.

4 Church St., was a Spirit Vaults occupied by 7 people: Robert Barr, 56, engine fitter and publican of Scotland; wife Jane 44 of Scotland; Dorothy of Hartlepool, 24; Grace, 19, dressmaker of Hartlepool; John, 13; and Mabel, 9 of Workington; and Robert, 6, of Frizington.

5 Church St was a Co-Operative General Store. The local Co-Op movement started in Cleator Moor in 1858. Industrial work forced skilled workers into poverty, so tradesmen joined together to open their own store selling food they could not otherwise afford. Originally selling simple stuff like butter, sugar, flour, oatmeal and candles. Within a few months sales at co operative stores included tea and tobacco, and then providing high quality, unadulterated goods. By 1958 there were branches at Whitehaven, Bowthorn, Cleator, Moor Row, Ennerdale, Frizington, Rowrah, Wath Brow, Pica, Moresby Parks, Parton, Distington, Bransty, Kells, Bigrigg, Hensingham and St Bees as well as multiple stores on Cleator Moor.

6 Church St., was occupied by 5 people: Joseph Clements, 46, Ore mine labourer, from Cleator; Christina, wife, 45; and their children William, 18; Christina, 14; Joseph, 8.

7 Church St., was occupied by 3 people: Richard Jenkinson, carter, 27, of Beckermet; wife Martha, 21 of St Bees; and infant son Isaac, 1 year old born at Moor Row.

7A Church St., was occupied by 1 person: Elizabeth Warwick of Bromfield, 56, dress maker.

8 Church St., a drapers shop and post office, was occupied by 11 people: William Simon, 48, coal merchant and commission agent of Brigham; wife Jane, 46, draper of Prospect; and 9 children: Ann, 25, born Seaton; John, 25, coal merchant born Broughton Moor; Frank, 21, apprentice colliery manager born Great Broughton; Mary, 19, dress milliner of Whitehaven; Margaret, 16, apprentice dress maker, of Maryport; William, 14, of Broughton Moor; Selina, 12, of Ullock; Elizabeth, 10; Johnathan, 8 of Egremont.

9 Church St., was occupied by 5 people: Hannah Orr, 42, widow living off her own means; John, 17; William, 13 of Cleator; Dorothy Forsyth, 13 of Cleator; Hannah Poole, 22, of Whitehaven.

10 Church St., was occupied by 4 people: Ann Ward, 42, widow, of Whitehaven; Mary, 15; Margaret, 12; and Mary A Ward, niece, 10.

Moor Row Residents 1891- Organised By Streets.

11 Church St., was occupied by 5 people: Isaac Walker, 40, overman at iron ore mine, of St Bees; Annie, wife, 41; Isaac Walker, son and storekeeper, 17; Annie, 11 years old.

12 Church St., was occupied by 7 people: Andrew Thomas, 53, iron miner of St Just Cornwall; Louisa, 46, wife; William A, 20, painter; Athanasius, 18, joiner; Annie, 15; Mary, 13; Andrew jnr, 8.

13 Church St., was occupied by 3 people: James Shields, 53, railway signalman from Ireland; Hannah, wife, 40; Lizzie, 8.

14 Church St., was occupied by 4 people: William Jackman, 60, iron miner from Devon; Harriet, wife, 58; James, 26 labourer; Bessie, 19, housekeeper.

15 Church St., was occupied by 5 people: Margaret Cross, 43, widow, of Scotland; Margaret A, 22, assistant school mistress; Archibald, 17, iron mines clerk; Jane, 13; Edwin A Underhill, 21, boarder and assistant school master from Upper Gornal Worcestshire.

16 Church St., was occupied by 7 people: Tom A Braithwaite, 36, locomotive driver, of Everton; Marion, wife, 36; Marion, daughter, 10; Harry, 8; Ethel, 6; Elsie, 4; Fred S, infant. In 1881 Tom, Marion and the infant Marion lodged in Egremont Main St at Henry Ashley's house. In 1901 Tom and his family lived at number 9 Church Street in Moor Row with nine in the household: Tom, Marion, Harry, Ethel, Elsie, Fred, and then Nellie, Bridgit, Milikin, widow and mother in law, 76; and Emma Tiffin, 28, boarder and head mistress of a board school, from Bagrow.

17 Church St., was occupied by 4 people: John Jackson, joiner, 44; Susan, wife, 38; Sarah, 15; Charlotte, 6.

18 Church St., was occupied by 8 people: Joseph Fletcher, 43, railway traffic inspector from Flimby; Elizabeth, 44, wife from Ireland, William, son and iron miner, 19.

19 Church St., was occupied by 4 people: Edmund Smith, 37, Blacksmith of Hensingham; Elizabeth, 19, wife from Cornwall; Kate, aged 1.

20 Church St., was occupied by 7 people: Thomas Lancaster, 37, platelayer of Moresby; wife Mary, 29; John, 13; Mary, 11; Thomas, 6; William, 2; Henry, 1.

21 Church St., was occupied by 6 people: Jonathan Lucas, 34, locomotive driver; Elizabeth, wife, 32; Jonathan, son, 10; Sarah Ann, 8; George, 6; Elizabeth, 2.

22 Church St., was occupied by 8 people: William Anderson, 54, locomotive driver; Barbara, wife, 50; William, son, 27 locomotive stoker; James, 18, ore miner; Barbara, daughter, 16, servant; Thomas, 14; Hannah, 12; Barbara Wallace, grand daughter, 8. The Grand daughter Barbara Wallace is the daughter of Kenneth and Jessie Wallace (nee Anderson) who lived with William et al, at 'Concreet Row' Egremont in 1881, but in 1891 Kenneth and Jessie lived in 56 John Street with the three youngest of their children. William and Barbara also had a daughter, Bridget C born 1869 living at Egremont with the family.

23 Church St., was occupied by 5 people: Thomas Haugh, 45, iron miner Eleanor, wife, 51; Jane Jenkinson, daughter, 30 and single; Fanny Haugh, 20, dress maker; and Mary H Haugh, daughter and school teacher, 17. The 1901 census records all the children as step daughters.

24 Church St., was occupied by 2 people: Thomas McLaughlin, 61, iron miner; Sarah, wife, 53.

25 Church St., was occupied by 6 people: Jane Higgins, 49, widow; Joseph, son, builders accountant, 23; John, 21, ore mine labourer; Jonas L, 17, drapers apprentice; Mary, 15; Sarah J, 8. Mrs Higgins was widowed four weeks before the census was taken, when her husband

James died after being recovered from Stirlings Montreal Pit 10 having been trapped for 20 hours under a rock.[22]

26 Church St., was occupied by 6 people: Richard Watters, 60, iron miner from Sancreed Cornwall; Ann, wife, 58 also from Sancreed; Joseph, son, iron miner, from Sancreed, 22; Mary J Watters, daughter in law, 20 from Egremont; Thomas Kinnish, 24, son in law, ore miner from Hensingham; Sarah Kinnish, nee Watters, daughter, 26, wife, from Sancreed. The Watters elders and the Kinnish family moved to 54 John Street by 1901 with their grand daughters Mary and Lillian.

27 Church St., was occupied by 9 people: Thomas Robinson, 39, ore miner; Mary, wife, 35 from Patterdale Ireland; Isaac, 13; Elizabeth J, 11; Mary.9; Esther, 7; Sarah P, 3; Joseph, infant; Mary Garnett, widow and housekeeper, 64, of Greysouthern. In 1901 Thomas was living with four of the children and a new wife, Jane, from Carlisle at 106 Ennerdale Road.

28 Church St., was occupied by number 1 Scalegill Road, the two properties being joined together behind one door.

29 Church St., was occupied by 4 people: Ann Fee, 50, widow and shopkeeper from Distington; Sarah Fee, 17, domestic worker; George Irvin, 47, boarder and iron miner; Benjamin Drake, 21, railway engine cleaner. Benjamin Drake seems to have been the grand son of John and Margaret Bateman from Beckermet: John had two step sons from Liverpool, William and James Drake, living with them in 1861. By 1871 an infant Ben Drake was living with his grand parents. In 1861 Margaret Drake was a Mate's wife living in Woolfe Street Toxteth, with four children including the then 5 year old Joseph, plus Mary Denehy an Irish born house maid. It is possible that Margaret Drake married William Bateman of Beckermet.

---

[22] 'Sad Mining Accident at Moor Row' *Whitehaven News* 19th March 1891.

30 Church St., was occupied by 8 people: James Williams, 29, iron miner of St Just Cornwall; Sarah A, wife, 25 of St Erth Cornwall; William J, 8; Minnie, 7; Thomas C, 6; Ruth, 4; Henry, 2; Lottie, infant born 1891; all born Cumberland.

31 Church St., was occupied by 4 people: Richard Park, 24, iron miner from St Ives Cornwall; Margaret, wife, 22; Edward, 2; Peter, infant.

32 Church St., was occupied by the Moor Row Reading Room.

33 Church St., was occupied by 3 people: Lundie Wise, 57, joiner; Martha, 35, and wife; Jane, 16.

34 Church St., was occupied by 5 people: William Smith, 36, ore mine labourer; Sarah, wife, 35; Peter, 5; Elizabeth, 4; William, infant.

35 Church St., was occupied by 5 people: John Madden, 39, iron miner; of St Ives Cornwall; Esther, wife, 32;of Cleator Moor; Mary, 9; John, 5; Isabella, 3.

36 Church St., was occupied by 7 people: Athanasins Chapple, 36, contractor of Cornwall; Annie, wife, 30; John Chapple, father and widower, 70; Irene Chapple, 4,; Harry, 2; Annie, infant; Emily J Trevaskis, servant, 15, from Egremont.

37 Church St., was occupied by the Primitive Methodists Chapel.

Dalzell Street Moor Row in 1891

The Dalzell Street houses from number 7 to number 31 were built with four rooms only, literally two up and two down. A new objective for the 1891 census was to determine the degree of over crowding in houses with less than 5 rooms.

1 Dalzell St., the Railway Hotel, was occupied by 6 people: Matthew Barnes, 64, innkeeper; Isabella, daughter, 29; Henry Frearson, son in law, 32, bacon curer from Lancashire; Hannah Frearson, married daughter, 27; Joseph A B Bowes, grandson, 14; Mary Sewell, niece, 20.

2 Dalzell St., was occupied by 8 people: James Reed, 30, iron miner of Ireland; Elizabeth, wife, 26 from Cleator; George, 6; Elizabeth, 4; John, 1; Mary, infant baby; Thomas Reed, 27 lodger and iron miner from Ireland; William Steadman, 30, iron miner from Ireland.

3 Dalzell St. was occupied by 8 people: Ann O Neill, 52, widow; William O Neill, son, 29, iron miner from Ireland; Michael O Neill of Ireland, 27 iron miner; Mary O Neill of Ireland, daughter, 25, single; and four more Ireland sons, all iron miners- Edward, 23; James, 21; John, 19; Daniel, 17.

4 Dalzell St. was occupied by 3 people: Paul Langton, 26, iron miner of Ireland; Mary, wife, 30 of Ireland; Elizabeth, daughter, infant, born Egremont.

5 Dalzell St. was occupied by 6 people: James Davey, 32, carter from Cornwall; Isabella, wife, from Cleator, Thomas H, son, 4; James, 2; Elizabeth A, 1; Elizabeth Hall, mother, widow, 72.

6 Dalzell St. was occupied by 2 people: Jane Mossop, widow and grocer, 64 of Distington; Jane Mossop, daughter, domestic servant of Egremont.

7 Dalzell St. was a grocers shop.

8 Dalzell St. was occupied by 5 people: Isabella Cass, widow, 68; William Cass, son, 31, fitters labourer of Cleator; Mary Cass, wife, 38; Sarah Jane Turner, daughter, 15 of Hensingham; Isaac F Turner, 35, a retired farm worker.

9 Dalzell St., was occupied by 5 people: William Braithwaite, 31, railway guard from Bootle Cumbria; Dinah, wife, 29 of Cleator; John William, 7; Elizabeth, 3; Frances, infant.

10 Dalzell St., was occupied by 5 people: John Wright, 32, railway engine driver, of Whitehaven; Julia M wife, 29; Elizabeth A, 9, Evaline, 5; Edith, 2.

11 Dalzell St., was occupied by 3 people: Alexander Mitchell, 23, railway stoker, from Scotland; Bridgit, wife, 24 from St Bees; Mary, infant, born Egremont. By 1901 they were living at 71 Penzance Street with 3 children then 55 Penzance Street by 1911. Mary no longer lived with them by 1911, and they had a new son, Gordon born 1903. The eldest son, also Alexander and born 1894 was working as a locomotive apprentice fitter.

12 Dalzell St., was occupied by 2 people: John Jenkinson; 31 locomotive driver of Cleator; Elizabeth, wife, 28. Twenty years later, 1911, the couple lived at 1A Back Corkickle Whitehaven, with John working as a night storeman for the Furness Railway. In between, they lived at 33 Penzance Street in 1901.

13 Dalzell St., was occupied by 6 people: Robert Park, 32, iron miner; Annie, wife, 27; 4 children- John, 5; William, 4; Matthew, 2; Ann, infant. Robert was living in 108 Gray Street Workington in 1911, working as a coal man and carter with three of the seven children, having taken up work in 1900 as a coal miner. His two eldest had followed him down the pit by 1901 at 15 and 14 years old, when they were living at Bottom Bank Distington.

Moor Row Residents 1891- Organised By Streets.

14 Dalzell St., was occupied by 4 people: Thomas Jenkinson, 75, iron miner from Greystoke; Elizabeth, wife, 58 of Cleator; William Martin, stepson, 18 and iron miner from Gosforth; William Hewitson, lodger and bachelor, 53, working as a platelayer for the railway, from Aspatria. Williams older sister Francis Martin, born 1873, had worked as a dress maker from the family home in 1881.

15 Dalzell St., was occupied by 5 people: George Coward, 72, engine fitter from Ireleth Lancashire; Annie, wife, 77 from Corney; Annie, single daughter, 37, dressmaker from Ulpha; George Bowerbank, 28, grandson, painter working for the railway, from Ulverston; Annie Bowerbank, grand daughter, 24, domestic servant.

16 Dalzell St., was occupied by 4 people: William Elliot, 28 of Egremont, no occupation recorded; Dorothy Ann, wife, 24, occupation described as Joiner; Grace, daughter, 2; Archibald B, 1;

17 Dalzell St., was occupied by 7 people: John Newton, 32, iron miner; Isabella, wife, 28; 5 children- James, 7; Matthew B, 6; Ada, 4: Joseph, 2; George, 1.

18 Dalzell St., was occupied by 4 people: Henry Steele, widower, 59, iron miner of Gosforth, Margaret Steele, daughter, 30, dress maker of Egremont; Dinah, 28, school mistress, John, 25 grocers assistant; Henry's late wife was Mary, born 1836, from Distington. They lived at Moor Row Farm in 1881 with their three children.

19 Dalzell St., was occupied by 3 people: Martha McCann, 47, from Whitehaven; James McCann, 22, sewing machine agent; John Fyffe, 63, joiner at ore mine, from Scotland..

20 Dalzell St., was occupied by 2 people: John Mossop, 38, grocers assistant, of Hensingham; Elizabeth, wife, 29, Arlecdon.

21 Dalzell St., was occupied by 3 people: Joseph Jenkinson, 28, iron miner, and his two sons Henry, 2, and John, infant. Joseph had moved to Dryhurst Kinniside by 1901 with Elizabeth, then 40, as his wife, and an extra daughter, Elizabeth born 1896, with a servant, Elizabeth Gorley, 17. In 1911 the family of five had moved to a dairy farm at Winscales with Anastasia Davis, 18, of Cleator Moor working as a servant.

22 Dalzell St., was occupied by 2 people: John Eddy, 67, ore miner, of St Just Cornwall; Sarah, wife, 64, of Ludgvan Cornwall.

23 Dalzell St., was occupied by 6 people: John Jackson, 27, iron miner from Bootle Cumberland; Mary Jane, wife, 31; and four children- Mary Ann, 8; Tamar, 5; John J, 2; Frances, 1.

24 Dalzell St., was occupied by 5 people: Thomas Mossop, 35, carter; Mary, wife 27; three children- Isaac, 5; Christina, 3; James, 1.

25 Dalzell St., was occupied by 10 people: William Fargher, 42, iron miner from the Isle of Man; Margaret A, wife, 33, from the Isle of Man; John E Fargher, son, 16, iron miner;; and their 6 other children- Robert, 13; Mary E, 10; Forbes, 7; William, 5; Eleanor, 3; Margaret A, 1; Barbara Creer, Mother in Law, widow, 67, from Scotland. All the children were Cumberland born.

26 Dalzell St., was occupied by 8 people: Edward McCabe, 45, Stoker at blacksmith, of Ireland; Isabella, wife, 42 of Whitehaven; and 6 children- Christina, 17; Elizabeth, 14; Joseph, 10; James, 7; Douglas, 4; Annie M, 2. The McCabe family had moved to 6 Church Street with the three youngest children by 1901.

27 Dalzell St., was occupied by 8 people: John Jeffrey, 33, iron miner from Caldbeck; Mary A, wife, 32; William, 13; Richard, 10; George H, 9; Elizabeth, 7; John James, 5 Charles, 2. John, Mary, William and Richard had previously lived at Nook St Arlecdon in 1881 where he worked as an iron miner.

Moor Row Residents 1891- Organised By Streets.

28 Dalzell St., was occupied by 3 people: Patrick Reiling, 61, coal miner; Elizabeth, wife, 61; Elizabeth, daughter, 8. Ten years earlier the Reilings lived at 25, The Ginns in Whitehaven, with two married sons, two married daughters, 3 unmarried children and a lodger, Thomas Kellop who worked as a potter, 28. They all came from Crosscanonby except for Whitehaven born Patrick, Elizabeth and Robert. In 1871 the Reilings, or Reelings, were living as a family of ten at Crosby Villa Cross Canonby.

29 Dalzell St., was occupied by 7 people: John Milburn, 40, coal miner; Anne, wife, 28; Thomas, 7; James Robert, 6; Anne, 4; Charles, 3; Sarah J, 1. The family lived at Moor Row Farm in 1881.

30 Dalzell St., was occupied by 6 people: Joseph Sait, 37, iron miner from Parton; Mary J, wife, 28; Thomas, 6; Mary J, 5; William, 2; James, 2.

31 Dalzell St., was occupied by 7 people: Crispin Pharoah, 36, Miller; Elizabeth, wife, 36; five children- Joseph, 15; Mary J. 13; Hannah, 11; Isaac, infant; Tyson, infant. Crispin lived at Lamplugh Mill in 1881 with wife and three children and a lodger, the carter Thomas Roberts from Wales, 42. By 1901 the family had moved to 8 Blue Quarry Gateshead to work as a mine pump man.

32 Dalzell St., was occupied by 6 people: William Pattinson, 54, labourer on a farm, from Beckermet; Ann, wife, 53; Thomas Helling, stepson, mineral borer; Agnes Helling, step daughter, 22, dress maker; William, son, 12; Elizabeth R, 10. Thomas and Agnes lived at Cote Close farm Egremont in 1881, 103 acres, with William and Ann Pattinson and 2 more servants. Cote Close with Cobra Castle estate is where Velda Cook grew up with her sister Kristina. Velda moved to Moor Row Dalzell St. in 2002. Her dad Dr Harry Cook was capped for rugby union, researched animal nutrition and soil chemistry at university, and held high office in the National Farmers Union while negotiating with the European Union and UK Government. Her mother Patricia helped teach skating at the family rink in Manchester and she toured as a dance skater, being introduced to General Franco the Spanish head of state.

33 Dalzell St., was occupied by 6 people: Matthew Barlow, 40, ore miner of Ireland; Catherine, wife, 29 from Cumberland; four children- Mary Ann, 8; Elizabeth, 7; Margaret, 5; Sarah, 2.

33A Dalzell St., was occupied by 5 people: Joseph Robinson, 44, ore miner; Dinah, wife, 44; Ann, 13; John, 12; Jonathan, 8.

34 Dalzell St., was occupied by 2 people: George Dickinson, 64, retired railway signalman of Lancashire; Jane, wife, 54, dress maker from Cleator. In 1881 John Calvert, accountant, 20 lived with them.

35 Dalzell St., was occupied by 4 people: Daniel Wilkinson, 31, railway goods guard; Esther, wife, 34; Mary J, 8; George, 3.

36 Dalzell St., was occupied by 4 people: George Cockle, 27, railway engine stoker; Margaret, wife, 25; Jane, 2; Mary, infant.

37 Dalzell St., was occupied by 6 people: Hugh McDowell, 35, railway engine driver, from Caernarvonshire; Hannah, wife, 34, from Bootle Cumberland; four children- James, 11; Mary, 8; Henry S, 6; Annie, 3.. By 1901 Hugh was working as a locomotive driver and a magistrate, son James worked as a railway engine cleaner.. They had moved to 53 Dalzell Street with their four children and nephew, Samuel Briggs born 1886, working as a railway office boy and niece Agnes Briggs. The Briggs father, John, appears to have been a manager with the Co-Operative society in Workington and Arlecdon.

38 Dalzell St., was occupied by 9 people: Galnil Thomas, 45, ore miner from St Just Cornwall; Mary, wife, 5, from Madron Cornwall;,

William G, son, 21, ore miner; Harry, 15; Mary, 13; James, 11; Galnil, 8; Eliza, 6; Fred, infant.

39 Dalzell St., was occupied by 9 people: John Thwaites, 34, ore miner; Sarah A, wife, 33, of Irton; seven children- Elizabeth, 13; Joseph, 11; William, 10; Jane, 8; Albert, 6; Laura, 4; Louisa, 2.

40 Dalzell St., was occupied by 3 people: John Smith, 28, railway goods guards: Mary F, wife, 28; William, 1.

41 Dalzell St., was occupied by 4 people: Henry Adams, 28, ore miner; Sarah J, wife, 26; Mary, 4; Ellen, 1.

42 Dalzell St., was occupied by 4 people: Benjamin C Williams, 24, ore miner, from Ludgvan Cornwall; Matilda, wife, 24, from Gulval Cornwall; Benjamin J, son, infant born Egremont; Edith Williams, single sister, 19 from Ludgvan.

43 Dalzell St., was occupied by 7 people: John Atkinson, 43, ore miner from Alston. Jane, 51 wife, from Isle of Man; Robert Kinnish, stepson, 23, ore miner from Isle of Man; William Kinnish, 19, ore miner from Isle of Man; Birkett Bell, son in law, 21, ore miner from Isle of Man; Catherine A Bell, daughter, 21, from Isle of Man; Charles Kinrade, single, lodger, 43 from Isle of Man.

44 Dalzell St., was occupied by 4 people: Robert Wilkinson, 63, stationary engine operator from Ulverston; Jane, wife, 69, of Driffield Yorkshire; Robert Wilkinson, grand son of Egremont, 14; Frederick Wilkinson, grand son, 8, of Egremont. By 1901 Robert Wilkinson was working as an ore miner and married to Henrietta from St Bees. They had an infant son William A born 1900. Frederick Wilkinson still lived with them and worked as a stoker on a stationary engine. By 1911 Robert Wilkinson had moved his family to 1 Penzance Street, with new wife Elizabeth Cowly, 23, William A, 11; Tom Dixon, son, 9; Robert Wilkinson, son, 1; William Smith, uncle and widower, 50,

William Smith, cousin, 20, a fish hawker; Robert Smith, cousin, 18 ore mine labourer, George Smith, cousin, 15; Annie Smith, cousin, 13.

That's a total of ten people altogether in Number 1. Other census returns for 1901 suggest William Smith, then living at 151 Frizington Road Arlecdon, to be Elizabeth Cowley's father, meaning Smith became Robert's in laws. Frederick Wilkinson was boarding at 20 Dalzell Street in 1911 with James George Brereton and his family, and working as a weigh man at the ore mine.

45 Dalzell St., was occupied by 8 people: William James, 53, overman at ore mine, from Ludgvan Cornwall; Elizabeth, 50, from Ludgvan Cornwall; Richard James, son, 27, joiner from Egremont; Henry, 21, draper assistant, Elizabeth, 20, mothers help; Margaret, 13; Samuel, 11; Mary,8;

46 Dalzell St., was occupied by 2 people: John Nicholls, 61, retired iron ore manager, from Gulval Cornwall; Mary, 58, wife, from Lelant Cornwall.

In 1901 there were three residents at number 46: Mary Nichols, 68, widow, of Lelant Cornwall. Also, Jacob George, grandson and medical student born Frizington, and Fanny Wills, 29, servant from St Dennis Cornwall. By 1911 there were three new residents, Joseph Sumpton, 66, joiner from Hensingham and two daughters, Maggie, 22 and Bella, 14.

In 1939 there were eight residents: Sarah Lowery, 63, widow, Isabel Dawson, (nee Lowery), single, 21 an elementary teacher; Arthur Bewthwaite, 23, colliery onsetter, Lillian Woodrow, widow and unpaid domestic, 40, Vera Peters, 9, student; Norah Durkin, married, 24 and an unpaid domestic.

47 Dalzell St., was occupied in 1891 by 7 people: George Thomas, 34, ore miner from St Just Cornwall; Sarah, wife, 29; Mary S, 7; John, 5:

Sarah Jane, 3; James G, infant; James Young, 75, father in law, widower and retired master mariner of Harrington.

In 1901 Sarah McLauchlin was living at number 47 on her own means, a widow aged 63. In 1911, James Bailey was living at 47, 85 years old, a shop keeper and baker from Croft Top Waley Lancashire. Also, Mary Jane Bailey, 58, wife and assisting in the business from Towednack Cornwall.

By 1939, Martha M Higgin lived at number 47, a widow of 47 years old. Also Alfred Higgin, unmarried and a joiner of 22 years old; Esmie Higgin, later Corrie, aged 21, confectioner and cake maker. In 2002 Esmie Corrie sold number 47 to Dugald Lamb, scientist, and the house then passed to Velda Cook, purchasing manager, of Cobra Castle and Cote Close farms, Egremont.

48 Dalzell St., was occupied by 2 people: John Webb, 52, boot and shoe dealer, of Gwennap, Cornwall; Sidwell, wife, 45 from Gulval Cornwall. In 1881 their son John H Webb also lived with them, working as a clock maker and mender. There was also a boarder, Mary J Martin from Cornwall, aged 9.

49 Dalzell St., was occupied by 3 people: Joseph Baragwanath, 61, time keeper at ore mine, from Cornwall; Mary, wife, 60, from St Ives Cornwall; John, son, 28, theological student from St Ives.

50 Dalzell St., was occupied by 7 people: John Fairburn, 57, ore miner, from Scotland; Francis, his wife, from Cleator; George, 19 black smith; Annie, 16; Joseph W, 11; Frances, 8; and George W Fairbairn, boarder, 37, ore miner of Sancreed Cornwall.

In 1901, 5 people lived at number 50: Frances Fairbairn, now widowed aged 60. with Joseph W. Fairbairn her son who was single and worked as an ore miner aged 21. Also, Frances Fairbairn, single daughter aged 18 lived with them, along with Lancelot Mossop, aged 27, a railway engine fitter who was married to Annie Mossop, nee Fairburn daughter aged 26.

In 1911 William Henry Clitheroe, a 26 year old wagon fitter for the Furness Railway from Barrow in Furness was living at the house with his wife Frances, 28, from Moor Row; and an infant baby whose name was not recorded on the census of 1911.

1939 6 people occupied number 50: William H Clitheroe was working as an Oxy Cetylene Burner still living at number 50 with his wife Frances Clitheroe and their daughter Frances F Thompson, born 26 Mar 1911 married to Wilfred Thompson, an ore miner born June 1908.. Two other people also shared the house, whose names were redacted from the 1939 survey as of 2022.

51 Dalzell St., was occupied by 4 people: Richard Herr, 26, draper of Scotland; Martha, wife, 24 of Cleator; Alphonso, son, 1; and Elizabeth Bennetts of Egremont, domestic servant.

52 Dalzell St., was occupied by 5 people: John Calvert, 30, life insurance agent, of St Bees; Mary, wife, 26; William, 9; Joseph D., &; Jackson, 5.

53 Dalzell St., was occupied by 7 people: Joseph W Jee, 36, railway traffic inspector; Elizabeth, wife 34 from Scotland; Margaret A, 10; Mary E, 7; Janet B., 5; John B., 4; Joseph, 1.

54 Dalzell St., was occupied by 7 people: Joseph Dickinson, 47, railway locomotive painter from Whitehaven; Margaret, wife, 47; Hannah, daughter, 21; Isaac, son, 20, painter compositor; Joseph, son, 18 railway clerk; Sarah E, daughter, 17, school teacher, Alfred E Dickinson, 8.

55 Dalzell St., was occupied by 3 people: Margaret Bell. 68, widow of Scotland; Thomas, son, 24, ore mine clerk; and Harriet, 25 wife to Thomas, from Rotherham. Margaret was already widowed at the time of the 1881 census, when she was living with her three children and the boarder William Brown, 26 of Lanark, who worked as a mining engineer.

56 Dalzell St., was occupied by 5 people: William Lawson, 40, railway platelayer from Cleator; John James, son, 14; Henry, 11, son; Dinah, 8, daughter; Emily, 5, daughter.

57 Dalzell St., was occupied by 3 people: Mary Barry, 51, widow of Whitehaven; Charles, son, 19, railway engine stoker; Jonathan, son, 15, blacksmiths labourer.

58 Dalzell St., was occupied by 3 people: Sarah Forrester, 69, widow, house keeper of Egremont; William, son, 30, engine fitter; Deborah, daughter, 27, assistant school mistress. Deborah was listed as a school mistress in 1901, and single. John F., grandson of Sarah and 15, of Arlecdon, also lived at number 58 in 1901.

59 Dalzell St., was occupied by 7 people: Adam Bell, 54, ore miner, of Ulverston; Elizabeth, wife, 55; Mary A., daughter, 19, dress maker; Joseph D., 18, son, clogger; Thomas H., 13; Agnes, 10; and grand daughter Margaret A., 5. All the children having been born in Egremont.

60 Dalzell St., was occupied by 4 people: Anne Mossop, living on her own means, 49 of Gosforth; Ben P, son, 24, grocers assistant of Cleator; John Ben, son, 20, wine and spirit apprentice; Lancelot W, son, 17, engine fitters apprentice. By 1901 Lancelot had moved to number 50 Dalzell Street to live with his wife Annie (nee Fairburn of Egremont), and her widowed mother Francis, then aged 60, and Annie's brother Joseph a 21 year old ore miner and sister Francis (born 1883).

61 Dalzell St., was occupied by 2 people: John Wilson, 46, railway plate layer, of Hensingham; Hannah Wilson, wife, 40, from Distington.

62 Dalzell St., was occupied by 4 people: John D Bell, 26, railway clerk of Cleator; Mary E., wife, 29; Archibald, son, 2; Hugh C., infant.

63 Dalzell St., was occupied by 5 people: John Mitchell, railway platelayer, 54, of Scotland; Martha, wife, 50 of Scotland; Robert, son, 16, ore miner; Martha, daughter, 12; George Wood, 64, boarder, labourer, from Scotland.

64 Dalzell St., was occupied by 10 people: James Irving, 39, ore miner of Blencogo; Ellen, wife, 40; Thomas, 17; John, 12; Archie, 10; Jane, 8; Mary E., 5; James, 2; William, infant; Thomas Pearson, single, 30 of Whitehaven, a railway platelayer.

65 Dalzell St., was occupied by 8 people: Joseph Syson, 39, watchmaker, of Egremont; Isabella, wife, 36; Joseph, 16; William, 12; Isaac, 9; Annie, 7; John, 6; Robert, 1.

66 Dalzell St., was occupied by 4 people: John Barlow, 46, over man at ore mines, from Ireland; Elizabeth Barlow, wife, 47 from Scotland; William, son, 8, from Scotland; Michael Barlow, 37, boarder from Ireland, stationary engine man.

Fishers Court in 1891

Fishers Court is not identified on contemporary OS maps for the area. The households comprised three or four room dwellings. The property numbers below were used in the 1891 record, set down between the pages for the Railway Station with Station Terrace, and High Moor Row farm and Moor Row farm.

1 Fishers Court was occupied by 4 people, Ralph Vivian, 21, iron miner of Caldbeck; Mary, wife, 20 of Scotland; Ralph M., son, 1; and John M., infant, son. Ralph was the son of Ralph Vivian senior (born 1844), iron ore miner of St Austell, Cornwall and his wife Louisa (born 1835) also from Cornwall.

In 1881 Ralph and Louisa lived at 'Moor Roe' with Thomas Vivian, another son who was then 20 also from St Austell and Ralph, junior, then 11; and Marmaduke Edmonds, an iron miner from Brege in Cornwall; and Frederick Thomas, 31, an iron miner from Cornwall.

In 1901 Ralph junior's wife, Mary, the daughter of John and Martha Mitchell of Forfar in Scotland was living with her parents at 63 Dalzell Street in Moor Row, along with another Mitchell daughter Martha Mower (b 1879) who had married Edwin Mower, and also their adopted daughter Elizabeth Smith (b 1893). Also the Vivian grand children Ralph, 11; John M, 10; Robert M, 8; G W, 6; Mary infant; and their Mower grand children John M, 3; and Ralph M., infant. That's twelve in all in the one house at number 63.

By 1911 John Mitchell, then 73 and retired as a platelayer on the railway, still lived with Martha his wife, then 70. They shared house with six from the Mower family, Edwin, 34, ore miner, daughter Martha and wife to Edwin, then 32, and their children John, 13; Ralph McDonald, 10;George, 6; and Alice, 1, making eight in all.

2 Fishers Court was occupied by 5 people, John Sheehan, 52, of Ireland; Sarah, wife, 48, of Ireland; Catherine Sheehan, daughter, 25, factory hand; John, son, 18, ore miner; May E., 13, daughter. The family formerly lived at 13 Church Street Cleator in 1881.

3 Fishers Court was occupied by 4 people, James McAvoy, 31, iron miner from Down, Ireland; Jane, wife, 29, of Down Ireland; Annie, daughter, 2; John, son, infant. In 1881 James had lived at 52 Birks Road Cleator with his widowed mother Ann McAvoy of Ireland (born 1843), along with his three brothers and three boarders from the Burns family. Five of the seven at Birks Road were miners and two were scholars.

By 1901 James and Jane were living at 29 Dalzell Street with six children of their own, the youngest called James was born 1901.

4 Fishers Court was occupied by two people, Thomas Paterson, 28, railway engine stoker of St Bees; Jane, wife, 27 of Scotland. Thomas and Jane had moved to 5 John Street by 1901 and John was working as a locomotive driver.

Homesteads

One household that disappeared from census returns is Low Moor Row, shown on the 1863 Ordnance Survey on what is now Church Street and occupied in 1891 by John Garnett, a 24 year old iron miner, and his family Polly, wife, 23; William, 6; Hugh, 4; John, 2.[23]

High Moor Row was occupied by 4 people, Esther Hitchin, 50, widow and housekeeper, from Narberth Pembrokeshire; George W Hitchin, son, 16, labourer, of Egremont; John Wills, labourer and servant from Distington; Sarah Ward, 19, servant.

Moor Row farm buildings were occupied by 5 people, Henry Hartley, 51, widower and land proprietor, of Haile; William, son, 25, labourer of Gosforth; Margaret Wilkinson, 21, servant; Alfred Hodgson, 22, servant; John Fearon, 15, servant.

Low Moor Row farm was occupied in 1891 by John Iredale, 48, unmarried land proprietor of Egremont; Hannah Armstrong, 19, niece; Hannah Vickers, 50 servant; Charles Postlethwaite, 24, servant; James Crears, 15, servant.

> In 1871 a John Iredale, then aged 60 and married to Ann, age 62 was living at a property called Moor Row farm with John Iredale, son, then 28 and Hannah, then 23, with three servants namely Mary Cowley (20), John Slack (25) and John Jackson (63).

---

[23] There were also two 'High Moorrow farms' at what became Hollins farm and Larch Court. Some rough buildings next to a well had been named Low Moor Row at the junction with Church Street by 1898. Farmers are notoriously lax when keeping records of property and animal holdings.

In 1881, John Iredale, now 38, was described as farming 90 acres with 3 labourers, occupied Moor Row farm with Mary Briggs (53 housekeeper), James Elland (21 servant) and Robert Scott (16, servant).

Gutterby in 1891

Gutterby is described as a homestead dated from 1690, converted in to a row of six cottages, standing between Moor Row and Woodend [Caine 1916, p7]. They were demolished in the 1960s. The houses were numbered in the 1891 census record. They each had a maximum of four habitable rooms. In all 26 people lived in six houses, having two bedrooms, a parlour and a kitchen. Social rank did not necessarily bring home comforts in this neighbourhood. There were no servants in the nearby Woodend home of Thomas Allen of Glamorgan, iron mine manager, living with his wife Harriet and five children aged 15 to 5 years old. But the widow Eleanor Lindow at Wood End House, aged 66 and living alone on her own means, kept the 27 year old Elizabeth Gavey as her domestic servant.

1 Gutterby was occupied by 5 people, Henry Armstrong, 36, a stationery engine operator of Cleator; Dorothy, wife, 35; Elizabeth, 7; William, 5; and Abie, 2.

2 Gutterby was occupied by 2 people, George Nelson, 53, blacksmith of Distington; Margaret, wife, 53.

3 Gutterby was occupied by 3 people, James Tyson, 30, ore miner of Hensingham; Edith, wife, 22; Joseph, son, infant.

4 Gutterby was occupied by 3 people, Henry Kelly, 48, ore miner of Isle of Man; Ann Jane, wife, 40 of Ireland; William Gaw, 75, father in law and hawker, of Ireland.

5 Gutterby was occupied by 6 people, John Hodgson, 37, stone mason of Torpenhow; Mary A, wife, 35; Jane, 7; Thomas, 5; Laura M, 1; Jane Reeves, visiting, aged 25 of Crosby Eden.

Moor Row in 1891

6 Gutterby was occupied by 7 people, Thomas Martin, 31, railway signalman, of Embleton; Margaret, wife, 35; Alfred, 1; John, infant; Thomas Partington, stepson, railway clerk, 16; Catherine Partington, widow and mother in law, 69; Catherine Richardson, niece, domestic servant, 18.

John Street Moor Row in 1891

In the 1891 Census there were 19 households recorded at numbers 1 to 12 and numbers 51 to 57 inclusive. The houses 13 to 50 were not recorded. The 1901 census recorded 34 households, then 39 in 1911 and 40 in 1939.

1 John St., was occupied by 3 people: William Copeland, 52, locomotive driver, of Whitehaven; Mary Jane, 55, wife from Ireland; William Copeland, son, 20, locomotive stoker.

2 John St., was occupied by 6 people: widower John Carron, 51, locomotive driver, of Whitehaven; John R Carron, son, 17; Charles, 13; Mary J, 12; Mary E., Carron, niece, 18, housekeeper; Jane A Carron, lodger.

3 John St., was occupied by 8 people: George Glover, 43, engine fitter, of Newcastle; Elizabeth, wife, 38 of Wigton; Mary A., 12; Eliza, 10; George, 7; Joseph D., 2; John, infant.

4 John St., was occupied by 2 people: John Fletcher, 47, engine fitter, of Dean; Ann, wife, 47 from Ireland.

5 John St., was occupied by 7 people: Thompson Weir, 34, locomotive driver of Whitehaven; Mary J., wife, 34, of Penrith; Mary E, 12; Esther J, 10; Alexander, 8; John, 6; Annie, 2.

6 John St., was occupied by 8 people: Joseph Syson, 39, locomotive driver, of Ravenglass; Mary, wife, 40 of Parton; Thomas Syson, son, 17, railway clerk; Agnes, 14; Esther E., 12; Laura E., 6; Eleanor, 4; Mary, 2.

7 John St., was occupied by 4 people: Aaron Hadwin, 48, stationery engine operator, of Whitehaven; Margaret, wife, 50; Mary E Hadwin, 15, dress makers apprentice; Herbert, 14.

8 John St., was occupied by 3 people: Thomas Postlethwaite, 44, blacksmith of Egremont; Mary Ann, 44, wife, of Ambleside; Herbert, 8. By 1911, Herbert Postlethwaite was working as an ore mine labourer, married to Elizabeth, 18, from Moor Row and they had baby Elsie with them, as well as his mother Mary Ann Postlethwaite: They were still living at number 8 John Street.

9 John St., was occupied by 4 people: Robert Forrester, 34, railway clerk from Penrith; Hannah, wife, 25 of Cleator; Ann E., 6; Ada R., infant.

10 John St., was occupied by 11 people: George Grundill, 37, locomotive driver, of Shildon, Durham; Mary A., wife, 34 of Whitehaven; Charles W, 13; Annie J., 12; Joseph, 11; Elizabeth C., 10; George, 9; John, 5; Ethel M., 3; Tom, 2; Mary, infant.

George Grundill and Mary had four extra children in the family in 1901: Hannah, (b 1893), Ruth (b 1895), Grace (b 1966), and Harold (b 1898). By then Charles W was working as a railway signalman; Annie was working as a domestic servant; Elizabeth B worked as a dressmaker; George B worked as a platelayer. Joseph (b 1880) was not listed in the 1901 census, meaning there were still fourteen people living in number 10 John Street.

11 John St., was occupied by 7 people: Joseph Fisher, 49, locomotive driver, of Brigham; Jane, 48, wife of Maryport; Sarah B., 15 apprentice dressmaker; John P., 13; William H., 11; Janet L., 9; Ada A.,7.

12 John St., was occupied by 7 people: Benson Myers, 46, locomotive driver of Whitehaven; Mary, wife, 42 of Ingleton; Richard, 19, railway clerk; John M., railway porter; Thomas B., 15, railway parcels porter; Mary, 13; Robert H., 5.

[Numbers 13 to 50 were not recorded in the census of 1891 for John Street Moor Row.]

51 John St., was occupied by 6 people: Thomas Williams, 36, ore miner from St. Ives Cornwall; Ellen, wife, 38 from Cornwall; William J., 12, from Egremont; Herbert, 9; Winifred, 2; Clara, infant.

52 John St., was occupied by 7 people: Edwin Chapple, 44, joiner from Cornwall; Jane, wife, 32 from St Just Cornwall; Charles R., 17, school teacher from St Levan Cornwall; John J., 14, joiners apprentice, of Egremont; Athanasius, 12; Edwin, son, 8; Reumah, 3.

53 John St., was occupied by 9 people: Bowman Kendall, 42, ore miner; Mary, wife, 37; Robert, 18, ore miner of Whitehaven; Hannah, 14 of Durham; Isaac, 10; John, 8; Jane, 6; Lena, 4; Thomas G., 1. In 1881 Bowman, Mary, and 4 children lived at 4 Fearon Street Egremont while he worked as an ore miner.

54 John St., was occupied by 8 people: Joseph Sumpton, 45, joiner and wagon builder, of Hensingham; Fannie, 39, wife, of Calder Bridge; John J., son, 16, boiler smiths apprentice, from Hensingham; Fannie, daughter, 14; Thomas W., 12; Agnes G., 9; Hannah E., 7; Maggie, 2.

In 1881 Joseph, Fannie and three children lived at Garden Villa Hensingham, also with Peter Blair, 29, ore miner from Scotland and his wife Frances, 30 (b 1851) of India Qulion.

55 John St., was occupied by 4 people: John Roche, 30, iron miner of Ireland; Margaret, 28, wife from Ireland; daughter Ann, 4, of Ireland; Joseph Coulston, boarder and ore miner of Cleator Moor.

56 John St., was occupied by 5 people: Kenneth Wallace, 33, ore miner of Isle of Man; Jessie, wife, 28 of Egremont; William, 6; Alexander B., 4; Jessie, daughter, 1.

57 John St., was occupied by 5 people: William Brown, 33, grocer, of Egremont; Annie, wife, 28; John, 6 of Distington; Norman, 4; James

Lyver, nephew, 8, of Maryport.

William Brown's father was John Brown (b 1832) and worked as an ore miner in Moor Row. John was living in Church Street Egremont in 1861 with his wife, two sons and a lodger from Carlton (the widower William Stale, born 1871). By 1881 John had seven in his 'Moor Roe' household and a lodger, the accountant William Hannah (b 1858), and William Brown was working as a grocer.

Penzance Street Moor Row in 1891

1 Penzance Street was occupied by 6 people: John A Fee, 28, locomotive fireman of Hensingham; Esther E, wife, 27; Susan, 6; William, 4; Florence A., 2; Ann G., infant.

John A Fee's widowed mother, Ann, was a grocer in Moor Row in 1881, looking after John and Sarah, and two lodgers, Thomas Grundy, 24, a locomotive stoker and Joseph Grundil, 25 a locomotive driver. Ann had been married to William in 1871, living in 'Moor Roe' with three children, Joseph W., Martha A., and John A., then 8 years old.

By 1891 Ann, then 50, and her then 17 year old daughter Sarah had moved to Church Street Egremont to keep a shop. They also had taken in two boarders, Benjamin Drake, 21, of Beckermet who worked as a locomotive cleaner, and George Irvin of Whitehaven 47, an ore miner.

2 Penzance Street was occupied by 8 people: James Crears, 57 and locomotive stoker; Ann, wife, 47; William, son, 24, locomotive stoker; James, son, 18, iron miner; and four daughters- Hannah, 12; Ann, 10; Elizabeth, 6; Alice, 5.

3 Penzance Street was occupied by 2 people: Philip Palmer, 30, iron miner; Hannah, wife, 28.

4 Penzance Street was occupied by 7 people: Isabella Thomas, widow, 42, dress maker; William Thomas, son, 19, wagon fitter; Alfred F, 16, ore mine labourer; Justus A., 14, an iron mongers apprentice; Marina, 12; Isabella, 10, Herbert W., 5.

Isabella was a widow in 1881 with five children, all under 10 years old. The census records her overnight visitors on the day the enumeration was made as John Thornburn, 25, a local Methodist preacher, his wife Betsy, 25, and their daughter Hannah, aged 4. Isabella may have been the Isabella Thomas who was living in 'Moor Roe' in 1871 and married to Henry, born 1846, from Cornwall and their one year old daughter Sarah J.

In 1901, then 52 year old, Isabella was still living at number 4, with her bereaved son William, working as a carriage and wagon examiner; Justus, 24, a railway clerk, Marion, 22; Isabella, daughter and pupil teacher at board school; and Herbert W., 15.

5 Penzance Street was occupied by 5 people: Mary Jane Trevaskis, 47, widow and house keeper of Helston Cornwall; James, 13; Eliza, 10; William Trevaskis, nephew, 19 ore mine labourer, of Ludgvan Cornwall; Elizabeth J Thomas, sister in law, 48, widow and dress maker, of Ludgvan; Calenda Berryman, boarder, 64, widow and dress maker of Ludgvan.

6 Penzance Street was occupied by 7 people: William Armstrong, 59, retired ore miner of Frizington; Sarah, wife, 55; Joseph, son, 32, locomotive driver; John, 30, stationery engine operator; William, 22, ore miner; James, 19, stationery engine man; Thomas, 15, shoe makers assistant.

7 Penzance Street was occupied by 4 people: Thomas Muncaster, 28, iron miner; Eliza, wife, 28; John S., 3; Archibald Wood, boarder, 71, widower and tailor from Scotland.

In 1881, Archibald, already a widower, had retired from working as a railway guard and was living at Beckermet with daughter Mary (born 1846 at Carlisle) and her husband Henry Rothery, a master joiner who employed two boys. Henry and Mary had an infant son

Clement born 1881. Henry and Mary also had a nurse/ servant, Christina McCurdy, 18, of Birmingham and an apprentice joiner also called Clement (Nichol), 18, of Gosforth.

By 1891 Henry was married to Sarah (born 1842) and had an extra son James Rothery, born 1879.

In 1901 Thomas Muncaster and Eliza had moved to 61 Dalzell Street with their son Joshua, born 1892 and a boarder Clement Rothery, then 20, and working underground as a labourer in an ore mine.

8 Penzance Street was occupied by 8 people: James Nicholls, 55, ore miner from Cornwall; Mary Jane, wife, 52, from Maldron; Adelaide, 17, daughter of Cleator; Stephen, 13; John, 12; Richard, 9 all of Arlecdon. Also, their daughter Jane, 20, and her husband James Jenkins, 22, an ore miner, were living with them.

In 1881, James and his five siblings had been living in Moor Row with their parents John, an ore miner from Cornwall born 1857, and Rachel born 1852 from Scotland.

9 Penzance Street was occupied by 8 people: John Jackson, 49, stationery engine man from Workington; Sarah A., wife, 41; Mary J., 20 dressmaker; George S., son, 15, stationery engine firemen; Elizabeth, 13; William H., 11; Fanny, 8; John, 5;

John, Sarah and the four eldest children had been living at Stainburn in 1881.

10 Penzance Street was occupied by 3 people: William Greenaway, 31, iron miner from Italy; Margaret, wife, 28 from Ulverston; William S., son 3.

In 1881 William senior was living with his parents in Moor Row- Thomas, an ore miner, born 1831 of Henham Gloucestershire and his mother Ellen born 1828 in Whitehaven.

11 Penzance Street was occupied by 6 people: John Wilson, 25, blacksmith from St Bees; Elizabeth A., wife, 24, from St Just Cornwall; John R, 3; Ethel, 2; William C., infant. Also Robert Wilson, 57, John's father, a widower and ore miner of St Bees.

Robert Wilson had previously lived at Finkle Street St Bees in 1871, and in 1881 he worked as a stone mason and lived at Finkle Street, with Jane, his wife born 1840, and their sons John who worked as a farm servant and David, born 1868.

12 Penzance Street was occupied by 12 people in 1891: Wilson Wright, 51, ore mine overman of Sunderland; Sarah, wife, 46 of Cornwall; Sarah J., 21, domestic servant of Asby; Joseph, son, 18, ore mine labourer born Flookburgh; Mary E Thomas, step daughter, 17, domestic servant from Egremont; John, 13; Rhoda, 9; Ada, 9; Dorothy, 7; Dora, 7; George, 5; Fred, infant.

In 1901 their son William J, then 23, had also moved in from Cartmel and was working as an ore miner. Meanwhile Dorothy was working as a school teacher, Mary Thomas, John, Rhoda, Ada and George had moved out, and grand daughter Dorothy Tonge, born 1899 in Bolton Lancashire, was living with her grand parents.

13 Penzance Street was occupied by 3 people in 1891: Margaret Hoskings, 65, widow of St Just Cornwall; John, son, 33, ore miner of St Just; Mary E Daniel, grand daughter, 15 of Egremont.

Mary Daniel's father James Daniel had been a boarder with William and Margaret Hosking in St Just and their four children in 1871. By 1881 the widowed Margaret was living in Penzance Street Moor Row with John Hoskings, her son of 23; James, son, 21; Willie Veal, boarder, 18, who had lodged with the Hoskins in St Just; John T Mathews, grand son, 8; and John Row, 27, of Cornwall. John and his mother were living at 43 Dalzell Street Moor Row by 1901, and

Moor Row Residents 1891- Organised By Streets.

John, then 43, was working as a draper.

14 Penzance Street was occupied by 11 people in 1891: John Trembath, 42, ore miner of Morrah Cornwall; Elizabeth, 50, wife of Zennoe Cornwall; John, son, 17, of St Just Cornwall; Elizabeth, 15; James, 14; Eliza, 13; William H., 11; Mary, 9; Thomas E., 7; Mark D., 5; Matthew, 4; all the children born in Egremont.

In 1881, John was married to Margaret (born 1849) of St Just, and living at 37 Montreal Street Cleator with the five oldest children listed above.

15 Penzance Street was occupied by one person in 1891: Ann Rogan, 58, widow of Ireland. Ann was still living alone at number 15 in 1901, 'living on own means'.

She was living in Moor Row in 1881 with her husband John Rogan, a labourer from Ireland born 1831, and their son James, then 30 who worked as an ore miner. Also in 1881, Patrick Meghan boarded with the Rogans, a 30 year old stationery engine operator from Ireland.

16 Penzance Street was occupied by 10 people in 1891: John Jenkins, 44, iron miner of Penrhyn Cornwall; Rachel, wife, 39 from Scotland; John, 19, iron miner; William, 13, iron miner; and Elizabeth, 15; Alice, 11; Rachel, 9; Henry, 7; Samel, 2; Ellen, infant.

17 Penzance Street was occupied by 6 people in 1891: John Moffat, 51, iron miner of Dean Cumberland; Esther, wife, 44; 'TW', son, 25, railway guard; Jane, 20, daughter, dressmaker; Isaac, 13; James, 10.

18 Penzance Street was occupied by 5 people in 1891: David Wilson, 23, iron miner of St Bees; Sarah Jane, wife, 19; Jane, infant daughter; Daniel Little, 22, boarder and iron miner of Hensingham with Mary Little his wife, 22.

19 Penzance Street was occupied by 6 people in 1891: Charles Adams,

31, iron miner of Arlecdon; Nancy, wife, 30; Mary, 8; Elizabeth, 7; Joseph, 3; Christiana, 1.

20 Penzance Street (sic) had no recorded occupants in 1891.

21 Penzance Street (sic) was occupied by 2 people in 1891: 'Thomas Graham, 52, iron miner of Cumberland; Barbara, wife, 48'. This entry might be an error on the census, and could actually be for number 20

21 Penzance Street (sic) was occupied by 5 people in 1891: Richard Cornish, 31, iron miner,; Sarah A., wife, 25; Elizabeth, 7; William, 4; Eveline, 1.

22 Penzance Street was occupied by 8 people in 1891: Robert Briggs, 36, stationery engine man, of Whitehaven; Elizabeth, wife, 35, from Middlesex; Thomas, 14; William, 12; James, 10; Henry, 6; Richard J Walters, stepson, 4 of Egremont; William H Stevens, boarder, 20, iron miner of Breage Cornwall. In 1881 Robert lived in Arlecdon with his then wife Eleanor, born 1858, and the three eldest children.

23 Penzance Street was occupied by 9 people in 1891: Jane Richardson, married, 41, of Cleator; John, son, 15, fireman of stationery engine; Mark, 13, farm worker; Hannah, 22; Emily, 11; Thomas, 7; Margaret, 4; Ethel, 2; Eveline, infant.

> In 1871 Jane looks to have been marrried to William Richardson (born 1847) of Lancashire and living at Ingwell View in Egremont with Hannah and Mary J., a second daughter. By 1881 Jane, and her children Hannah 12, Mary 10, Sarah 8, John 5, Mark 3 and Emily one year old were living at Scalegill with Jane Gambels, 66, her widowed mother of Workington. Jane gave her occupation as 'charwoman' at Scalegill.

24 Penzance Street was occupied by 2 people in 1891: Isaac Gunson, 24, railway clerk of Arlecdon; and Jane W., 25, wife.

Moor Row Residents 1891- Organised By Streets.

In 1881 Isaac was living with his grand parents Isaac, blacksmith and Sarah Huddart in Arlecdon. Isaac Gunson worked as a railway clerk there at age 14, having earlier lived at Bolton le Sands in Lancashire with his parents Joseph and Jane and brother and sister Ann and William.

In 1901 Isaac, Jane and their two children had moved to 66 North Road Egremont where he worked as the station Master.

25 Penzance Street was occupied by 12 people in 1891: William Bryan, 34, boiler maker; Mary, wife, 33; and ten children, Jane R., 12; Isabella, 11; Elizabeth, 10; Edward, 9; Mary, 8, Maggie, 7; Stephen, 6; Nelly, 4; William, 2; Sarah H, infant.

By 1901 William and Mary had moved to 68 Penzance Street. Jane was then working as a dress maker, Edward a railway locomotive cleaner, and Stephen a railway clerk. They had an extra four sons by 1901, Henry, 8; Tom, 7; Albert, 5; John, 3. Mary and Maggie are not recorded as living at number 68, which housed 12 people in 1901.

26 Penzance Street was occupied by 6 people in 1891: Joseph Fee, 36, iron miner from Hensingham; Ann, 36, wife; Mary J, 12; James, 10; John, 7; Margaret, 5.

27 Penzance Street was occupied by 4 people in 1891: John Rowe, 36, iron miner from Sancreed Cornwall; Charity, wife, 31; Mary Rowe, mother, 73, living on own means; Thomas Rowe, brother, 23, iron miner. By 1901 John and Charity had moved to 11 Penzance Street.

28 Penzance Street was occupied by 3 people in 1891: Jakeh Glasson, 32, iron miner of Lelant Cornwall; Annie, wife, 36 of Gwinear Cornwall; John, son, 4, of Egremont.

29 Penzance Street was occupied by 6 people in 1891: John Nicholson, 36, stationery engine operator of Irton; Sara A., wife, 32 from Cleator; Isaac, 10; Mary J., 8; Joseph W., 5; Sarah A., infant.

Moor Row in 1891

30 Penzance Street was not listed in the 1891 census.

31 Penzance Street was occupied by 4 people in 1891: Isaac Nicholson, 29 stationery engine operator from Irton; Dorothy, wife, 25; William, 4; Elizabeth, 1. Isaac, Dorothy and their four children were living at Cleator in 1901.

In the first listing for 32 Penzance Street there were 6 people in residence in 1891: Isaac Nicholson, 63, mine labourer from Gosforth; Elizabeth, wife, 63; Eleanor Dixon, daughter and widow, 39 of Irton; Isaac Dixon, grand son, 13 of Egremont, William Nicholson, son, 25, stationery engine man. Also, Edgar Whitton, 24, Evangelist of Oswaldtwistle was visiting the house.

In the second listing for 32 Penzance Street there were four people resident in 1891: Eleanor Corkhill, 63, from Whitehaven; Sam Eilbeck, son in law, 31, mineral borer; Sarah E Eilbeck, wife and daughter, 29; Robert Eilbeck, grand son, 7; Sam Eilbeck, grand son, 4.

33 Penzance Street was occupied by 5 people in 1891: William Harrison, 33, stationery engine operator from Ulverston; Rebecca, wife, 32 from Cumberland; William, 9; Reuben, 6; Harold, 4 all from Egremont.

[Numbers 34 to 53 Penzance Street have no record in the 1891 census.]

54 Penzance Street was occupied by 2 people in 1891: Thomas Greenaway, 61, iron miner of Bristol, Eleanor, wife, 63 from Whitehaven.

In 1901 Thomas was living at 59 John Street as a widower and retired. He shared the house with his son William and William's wife Margaret with their children William, born 1888; and Eleanor A., born 1892.

55 Penzance Street was occupied by 9 people in 1891: John Murray, 46, a mineral borer from Scotland; William, son, 14 a labourer from Scotland; James, 11; Thomas, 10; Annie, 7; Jessie, 5; George, 2; Isaac, 1; and Mary Servant, 33, servant from Frizington.

56 Penzance Street was occupied by 6 people in 1891: John Selson,

39, blacksmith from Bothel; Hannah, wife, 39 from Frizington; Joseph, 15; Jane A., 14; William S., 13; Mary A., 5.

57 Penzance Street was occupied by 3 people in 1891: James Maddern, 42, iron miner from Madron Cornwall; Mary E, wife, 44 of Redruth Cornwall; Elizabeth Rodgers, sister in law, 42 of Cornwall.

By 1901 James and Mary had moved to 37 Dalzell Street.

In 1901 three new residents were living at 57 Penzance St: John Hogg, 54, ore pit blacksmith from Carlisle; Martha, 55, wife of Great Orton; son Thomas, 25, ore miner born Frizington. In 1911 John Hogg and Martha still lived at number 57 with Betsy Ore, widow of Great Orton.

In 1939 there were two residents, William Myers, an ore mine labourer and his wife Mary Myers. In 1921 Mary and William had been living in Yorkshire North Riding.

58 Penzance Street was occupied by 3 people in 1891: Edward Carson, 42, stationery engine driver from Whitehaven; Mary, wife, 47 from Cockermouth; James, son, 12.

59 Penzance Street was occupied by 3 people in 1891: John Davidson, 48, iron miner from Alston; Dinah, 44, wife from Penrith: Ernest Marshall, stepson, 20 from Ainsdale Lancashire, stationery engine fireman.

60 Penzance Street was occupied by 2 people in 1891: William Tee, 24, stationery engine operator, from Harden Durham; Hannah, 20, wife, from Egremont.

61 Penzance Street was occupied by 8 people in 1891: Thomas Todd, 49, stationery engine operator from Whitehaven; Margaret, 43, wife; Thomas Todd junior, son, 22, platelayer; George Todd, son, 18, farm labourer; Elizabeth, 14: Helen, 12; William, 10; Albert, 8.

62 Penzance Street was occupied by 6 people in 1891: John Graham, 36, iron miner from Ireland; Sarah, 46, wife from Egremont; Sarah Laidlaw, step daughter, 20, dress maker; Robert Laidlaw, step son, iron mine labourer; Hannah R Laidlaw, stepdaughter,12; Eliza Graham, 8.

62 Penzance Street also had a second entry showing 7 other people occupied the house in 1891: John Sumpton, 29; railway signalman from Hensingham; Ann, wife, 30 from Egremont; Mary A., 7; Gertrude, 3; Ada J., infant; John Nicholson, widower and brother in law, 30, railway signal man from Ravenglass; Martha Nicholson, boarder, 7, from Hensingham.

63 Penzance Street was occupied by 4 people in 1891: John Fletcher, 40, railway wagon works labourer from Flimby; Elizabeth, wife, from St Bees; Henry, son, 16, railway clerk; John, son, 14.

64 Penzance Street was not recorded in 1891.

65 Penzance Street was occupied by 5 people in 1891: Edward Wilson, 29,blacksmiths striker from Whitehaven; Mary, wife, 38; James McMehan, stepson, 16, stationery engine fireman from Egremont; Annie McMehan, step daughter, 14, from Egremont; Elizabeth Wilson, 2 from Egremont. In 1901 Edward, Mary and Elizabeth were living at 58 Penzance Street, and Edward was working as an insurance agent.

66 Penzance Street was occupied by 6 people in 1891: William Patterson, 34, locomotive fireman from St Bees; Mary Jane, wife, 28 from Egremont; John Joseph, 10; Elizabeth A., 8; William S., 2; Mary J., infant.

67 Penzance Street was occupied by 6 people in 1891: Joseph S. Pattinson, 38, locomotive fireman from St Bees; Mary A., 26, wife; Harrison, 7; Sarah, 4; Elizabeth, 2; Christopher W., infant.

68 Penzance Street was occupied by 6 people in 1891: Nancy Streck, 50, widow of Penzance Cornwall; Margaret J., daughter, 19 of Egremont;

Lydia, 15; Amelia, 11; Thomas Lowery, 18, boarder and stationery engine fireman from St Just Cornwall; Elizabeth Eddy, 80, widow and boarder of Madron Cornwall.

69 Penzance Street was occupied by 2 people in 1891: George White, 47, clogger from Maryport; Mary E., 44, wife.

70 Penzance Street was occupied by 7 people in 1891: James Strick, 39, iron miner of St Just Cornwall; Bessie, 35, wife of Sancread Cornwall; William, J., son, 15, ore mine labourer of Hensingham; Annie, 13; Charles, 11; Alfred, 8; George H., 5 all the children of Egremont.

71 Penzance Street was occupied by 4 people in 1891: Robert Cockbain, 69, stone mason from Whitehaven; Bridget, 75, wife from Scotland; John, son, 34 from Egremont; Sarah A., 20, grand daughter.

72 Penzance Street was occupied by 6 people in 1891: Robert Hope, 28, iron miner of Maryport; Sarah, 25, wife from Arlecdon; Jane Adams, daughter, 5, from Arlecdon; Robert Hope, 4; Joseph, 2; Mary A., infant, all the children of Egremont.

73 Penzance Street was occupied by 2 people in 1891: William Greenhow, 67, widower and iron miner of Mungrisdale; Hannah E Greenhow, 18, daughter from Cleator.

74 Penzance Street was occupied by 4 people in 1891: Edward Watson, 37, iron miner; Elizabeth, 39, wife; Bridget, 15, Robert, 4.

75 Penzance Street was occupied by 3 people in 1891: Joseph Graham, 34, locomotive driver; Mary J., 39, wife; Sarah A Dickson, 16, niece and pupil teacher from Whitehaven.

76 Penzance Street was occupied by 7 people in 1891: John Pearson, 43, railway wagon builder from Bridekirk Cumberland; Isabella, 41, wife from Whitehaven; Isaac Pearson, son, 18, stationery engine operator;

William, 16, stationery engine fire man; Hannah Pearson, daughter, 14; George, 6; Hannah Pearson, daughter, 4.

77 Penzance Street was occupied by 4 people in 1891: George Newton, 33, iron miner from Lamplugh; Barbara A., 32, wife from Gosforth; Thomas G., 12; James, 10.

78 Penzance Street was occupied by 6 people in 1891: John Brown, 59, iron miner from Beckermet; Ann, 58, wife; John, son, 23, railway signal man from Egremont; Jannie, 20, general servant; Hannah, 20, dressmaker; Ernest, 2.

> By the 1911 census John Brown was 80 years old and a widower living with his son in law Edward Thompson, iron miner from Dalton in Furness, and his wife Hannah Thompson (nee Brown) at 57 Main Street Frizington. Also, Edward and Hannah had two children, Annie, 13 and Norman, 9. Ernest Brown, now 22, also lived with them and worked as an iron miner. Number 78 Penzance Street was then occupied by Henry James from Bigrigg, 41, and his family of 5. Henry was working as an iron miner in 1911, having been a drapers assistant while living at 3, Mill Street Whitehaven in 1901.[24]

> By 1939, 78 Penzance Street was occupied by Isaac Jenkinson, 50, an ore mine pump operator, and his wife Agnes, also 50.

The Railway Houses

> **Alva House**, in the early 2010s was a boarding house. In 1891 railway traffic Superintendent William Postlethwaite, 45, of Dalton Lancashire, lived at Alva House with his wife, Margaret, 42, and their seven children: Francis, 19, railway clerk; Joseph W., 18, also railway clerk; Florence, 16, confectioners assistant; Elizabeth, 11; Edith, 10; George N., 7; Sarah A., 3. They previously lived at Grange Station House when William was station master for the railway, in 1881, having lived in Storey Square

---

[24] In 1911 there were approximately 1,500 iron miners in the Lamplugh- Whitehaven- Beckermet area, according to the census summary of that year.

Dalton in Furness in 1871 with the Titley family.

The Villas (1). was occupied by 4 people, John Wakefield, 54, Permanent Way inspector, of Kirklinton; Sarah, wife, 58, of Lamplugh; Faith, 29, daughter and school mistress of Loweswater; Catherine, 26, daughter, of Dean. The family had lived at Dean in 1871, then were living at Concreet Row, Egremont in 1881 when the two daughters worked as milliners assistants.

The Villas (2), was occupied by 9 people, Edwin Rose, 49, locomotive engine Superintendent from Staffordshire; Elizabeth, wife, 45 from Whitehaven; Annita, daughter, 22; George E J, 20, seaman; Frank E, 17 apprentice fitter; Arthur, 15; Ethel L, 10; Edwin, 11; Guy 5.

By 1901, Edwin and Ethel still lived at The Villas (renamed Victoria Villas), with Annette, Ethel, working as a school teacher, and Guy working as a locomotive engineer apprentice.

By 1911, Edwin and Elizabeth still lived with Annette (a possible transcription error for Annita) and Ethel.

Railway Station house, Moor Row Junction, was occupied by 5 people, Joseph Braithwaite, 46, station Master, Thomas W, son, 17, railway clerk; Isabella, daughter, 22, housekeeper; Thomas Bent, lodger and railway signalman, 49, of Whitehaven. John Bent, 14, a labourer was visiting at the time the census was taken.

In 1881 Joseph Braithwaite was working as railway station Master at Egremont, living with his wife Jane E., then 36, at the station, with; Mary, 10; Thomas W, 7; Emily E, 6; and Thomas Bent, 39, who was working as a railway porter.

Railway Terrace

1 Railway Terrace was occupied by 4 people in 1891: Catherine Redmond, 56, widow from Ireland; Patrick, son, 25, iron miner of Ireland; Peter, son, 16 of Cumberland; Dan, son, 14 of Cumberland.

Catherine was married to James Redmond, born 1839, and lived at Back Ennerdale Road, Cleator in 1871 with their family James, 10; Thomas, 7, Mary, 7. In 1881 they were living at 2 Ennerdale Road, with James, Thomas, Patrick, Peter, and Daniel, aged 4.

In 1901, Patrick, still an ore miner and still resident at number 1 Railway Terrace lived with Isabella (his wife) and their 6 children (James, 8; Mary, 6; Isabella, 4; Patrick, 2; Ellen, infant). Also Patrick seniors bother Peter, then 26, lived with them and he worked as an iron miner

By 1911 Patrick, Isabella and nine children were living at 17 Prospect Row Cleator (Isabella, Annie, Patrick, Nellie, Peter (9), Anthony (7), Thomas (4), Maggie (2) and John Joseph (infant). The two eldest daughters were then working as mill hands.

2 Railway Terrace was occupied by 5 people in 1891: William Murphy, 33, ore miner of Ireland; Elizabeth, 25, wife from Cumberland; Bridget, 5; Annie, 3; Teresa, 1.

By 1901 the family had moved to 32 Dalzell Street and grown with four more children: Elizabeth, 7; Agnes, 5; William, 2; and Richard, an infant.

In 1911 William and Elizabeth had four children living at their home in 32 Dalzell Street: Annie, a milliner; Elizabeth, Agnes, and William. Also two boarders, Thomas McAvoy, 44, a house painter from Preston, and Patrick Cavanagh, a house painter from Athlone, Ireland.

3 Railway Terrace was occupied by 8 people in 1891: Alexander Smith, 49, blacksmith; Jane, 43, wife; Isaac, 18, son and railway engine cleaner; Mary, 15, apprentice dressmaker; Ada, 12; Elizabeth, 10; Tom, 7; Mary, 4.

4 Railway Terrace was occupied by 4 people in 1891: Edward Ennis, 44, ore miner of Ireland; Elizabeth, 35, wife of Ireland; Denis Byrne, stepson and ore miner, 17, of Cumberland; Annie Byrne, 15, step daughter;. Edward and Elizabeth still lived at number 4 in 1911.

5 Railway Terrace was occupied by 2 people in 1891: William Elden, 23, ore miner of Cumberland; Elizabeth, 21, wife.

6 Railway Terrace was occupied by 2 people in 1891: William Butler, 32, ore miner of Scotland; Rose Ann, 24, wife, of Whitehaven.

Scalegill in 1891[25]

1 & 2 Scalegill, which together formed The Beehive Inn, was occupied by 8 people in 1891: Isaac Malcham, 44, publican and farm worker, from Clekheaton, Jane, 37, wife from Kentmere. They had five children between 15 and 2 years old. Also, Mary J Johnson, 28, a domestic servant from Cleator Moor.

3 Scalegill, was occupied by 5 people in 1891: Gardener Palmer, 28, iron miner; Mary Ann, 23, wife; two children aged 3 and 1; also Joseph Fisher, 18, labourer at iron mine,

4 Scalegill, was occupied by 4 people in 1891: John Brocklebank, 28, iron miner; Polly, 24, wife from Westmorland; and two children.

5 Scalegill, was occupied by 4 people in 1891: John Briggs, 28, iron miner; Elizabeth, 27, wife; and two children aged 2 and an infant.

6 Scalegill, was occupied by 4 people in 1891: Daniel McDonald, 45, iron miner; Catherine, 50, wife; and two children, Hugh, 18, iron miner, and Daniel, 14.

---

[25] The houses in Scalegill had four rooms in total, except for numbers 1 which was joined with 2, number 60 and number 63. In 1871 The Beehive Inn was listed in the census for Egremont as being on 'Ingwell View' with forty six other properties. Ingwell View returns were recorded between 'Shaw farm' and 'Moor Roe' on the original forms. Moor Roe included 'Station Hotel' and Victoria Villa.

7 Scalegill, was occupied by 8 people in 1891: John Cooper, 36, iron miner; Margaret, 36, wife; 5 children aged 11 to 2 years. Also, Thomas Nicholson, 25, boarder and iron miner.

8 Scalegill, was occupied by 10 people in 1891: William Heard, 39, iron mine labourer from Tiverton Devonshire; Sarah, 37, wife; eight children aged 15 to 1.

9 Scalegill, was occupied by 8 people in 1891: William Kirkbride, 57, iron miner of Distington; and five children, aged 24 to 14 and two grand children aged 5 and 1. Two of his sons were working as iron miners and the eldest daughter worked as a dress maker.

10 Scalegill, was occupied by 3 people in 1891: Jane Palmer, 24, and her two daughters aged 4 and 1.

11 Scalegill, was occupied by 2 people in 1891: Thomas Rowe, 21 iron miner from Cornwall and Ann Rowe, his grand mother, aged 65 from Cornwall.

12 Scalegill, was occupied by 6 people in 1891: Tom Vivian, 30, iron miner from St Austell Cornwall; Mary, 30, wife from Cleator; two children aged 7 and 5 and Mary J Williams aged 10, Tom's niece. Also Louise Vivian, Tom's mother from Cornwall, aged 57.

13 Scalegill, was occupied by 3 people in 1891: James Wilson, 48; Agnes, 50, wife; and Agnes Bushby, 10.

14 Scalegill, was occupied by 5 people in 1891: William Southward, 48, iron miner; Jane, 45, wife; John Southward, 22, son and iron miner; also 2 more children aged 12 and 10.

15 Scalegill, was occupied by 4 people in 1891: William Robinson, 26, platelayer, Jane, 26, wife; daughter Elizabeth, 6; and Ellen Gill, 50, mother in law and charwoman from Ireland.

16 Scalegill, was occupied by 3 people in 1891: Edward Bowness, 22,

Moor Row Residents 1891- Organised By Streets.

iron miner; Sarah Jane, 22, wife; William Briggs, widower aged 57, father in law and iron miner.

17 Scalegill, was occupied by 6 people in 1891: Sarah Fox, 28, lodging house keeper from Cleator Moor; two daughters aged 5 and 3; and 3 boarders named Robert Burns, 20, iron miner from Lincoln; Bertie Burns, 14, iron miner from Lincoln; Herbert Macham, 32, railway platelayer from Cleckheaton.

18 Scalegill, was occupied by 8 people in 1891: William Carruthers, 33, blacksmith from Liverpool; Mary, 29, wife from Egremont; six children aged 13, to infant.

19 Scalegill, was occupied by one person in 1891: Thomas Douglas, 64, grocer from Cleator.

20 Scalegill, was unoccupied in 1891.

21 Scalegill, was occupied by 3 people in 1891: George Cooper, 65, living on own means, from Westmorland; Hannah, 57, wife; also Thomas Barwise, 21, boarder and iron miner.

22 Scalegill, was unoccupied in 1891.

23 Scalegill, was occupied by 9 people in 1891: Richard Lowery, 60, iron miner from Muncaster; Maria, 57, wife from the Isle of Man; and seven children born Egremont, aged between 25 and 11. The three eldest sons, Isaac (25), David (21), and William (18) were iron miners.

24 Scalegill, was occupied by 4 people in 1891: William Thomas, 46, iron miner of St Ives, Cornwall; Mary A., 47, wife, of Sancreed Cornwall; and two children aged 12 and 9 of Cumberland.

25 Scalegill, was occupied by 2 people in 1891: James Palmer, 20, railway porter; Ann, 19, wife.

26 Scalegill, was occupied by 6 people in 1891: James Bewley, 41, joiner from Distington; Isabella, 30, wife; and four children aged 10 to 3.

27 Scalegill, was occupied by 8 people in 1891: John Laidlaw, 40, iron miner of Aspatria; Mary, 44, wife of Gosforth; and their six children aged 22 to 2 years old. The three eldest worked as iron miners and as a dressmaker.

28 Scalegill, was occupied by 7 people in 1891: William Wilson, 45, iron miner of Westmorland; Hannah, 36, wife from Gosforth; and their five children aged 15 to 1. The eldest, Moses (15), was working as an iron miner.

29 Scalegill, was occupied by 4 people in 1891: Richard Bennetts, 39, iron miner from Cornwall; Elizabeth, 30, wife, from Lelant Cornwall; and their two children born Cumberland aged 8 and 7.

30 Scalegill, was occupied by 6 people in 1891: Moses Hodgson, 36, iron miner; Ann, 33, wife; and their four children aged 7 to 2.

31 Scalegill, was occupied by 8 people in 1891: John Gray, 42, labourer from Ireland; Jane, 38, wife from Liverpool; and their 6 children aged 16 to infant.

32 Scalegill, was occupied by 3 people in 1891: Thomas Nicholson, 62, widow and iron miner from St Bees; and his two daughters aged 13 and 11.

33 Scalegill, was occupied by 5 people in 1891: John Pinder, 35, iron miner from Lancashire; Mary, 29, wife; and their three children aged 6 to 2 years old.

34 Scalegill, was occupied by 7 people in 1891: William Kelly, 45, iron miner from the Isle of Man; Ann, 45, wife; and five children aged 10 to 3 years old.

35 Scalegill, was occupied by 7 people in 1891: James Fisher, 52, from Hawkshead Lancashire; Jane, 49, wife from St Just Cornwall; and their three children aged 11 to 10 years old. William Tonkin (15) of

St Just, stepson to James, was working as a labourer in an iron mine, and Minnie Tonkin (11) born Egremont, step daughter to James also lived with them.

36 Scalegill, was occupied by 8 people in 1891: Felix Ward, 50, iron miner from Ireland; Mary, 49, wife from Ireland; and their six children aged 24 to 9. The two eldest, James (24) and Patrick (19) also worked as iron miners.

37 Scalegill, was occupied by 2 people in 1891: listed with one name 'Jefferson', 46, iron miner from Cleator Moor; and Mary A., 48, wife.

38 Scalegill, was occupied by 3 people in 1891: Edmondson Green, 50, labourer at iron mine from Papcastle; Jane, 47, wife from St Bees; Joseph Davison, 28, iron miner and lodger from Wigton.

39 Scalegill, was occupied by 3 people in 1891: Thomas Steele, 23, iron miner from Gosforth Cumberland; Elizabeth, 26, wife from Bridgefoot; and their infant son.

40 Scalegill, was occupied by 4 people in 1891: Thomas Nicholls, 21, iron miner; Annie, 22, wife; and their two children aged 3 and 1.

41 Scalegill, was occupied by 4 people in 1891: William Tredrea, 34, life assurance agent from Germoe Cornwall; Rosetta, 29, wife from St Ives Cornwall; and their two sons aged 7 and 6.

42 Scalegill, was occupied by 6 people in 1891: Anna May, 55, widow; John (21), locomotive fireman; Elizabeth (24); Isabella (17), a dress makers apprentice; Tom (12), and Lily (2).

43 Scalegill, was occupied by 4 people in 1891: Christian Thomas, 21, iron miner from Cornwall; Agnes, 21, wife; and their infant son William. Also, Edward Donnan, 17, brother in law to Christian, working as a warehouse man.

44 Scalegill, was occupied by 6 people in 1891: Henry Lowery, 35, iron miner, Eleanor 37, wife; and their four children aged 13 to 4 years old.

45 Scalegill, was occupied by 4 people in 1891: Robert Armstrong, 66, iron miner; Margaret, 52, wife; Joseph Johnstone, son in law, 22, iron miner; Isabella Johnstone, 22, stepdaughter to Robert and Joseph's wife.

46 Scalegill, was occupied by 2 people in 1891: William Wilson, 67, stationery engine man from Moresby; Mary, 64, wife from Moresby.

47 Scalegill, was occupied by 7 people in 1891: William Nanson, 49, farm servant, from Matterdale; Elizabeth, 31, wife from Dalton in Furness; and their five children aged 8 to 1 year old.

48 Scalegill, was occupied by 3 people in 1891: Tom Kirkbride, 28, joiner; Margaret, 24, wife; and their daughter Mabel aged 1.

49 Scalegill, was occupied by 5 people in 1891: William Johnston, 49, iron miner from Haile; Elizabeth, 44, wife from Gosforth; and their three children aged 20 to 12. William junior was born at Gosforth and worked as an iron miner, and Ann (20) worked as a dressmaker. Elizabeth (12) was born at Arlecdon. By 1901 William senior was still an iron miner, living at 157 Frizington Road Arlecdon with his wife Elizabeth.

50 Scalegill, was occupied by 5 people in 1891: Richard Kirkbride, 28, iron miner from Braithwaite; Eleanor, 31, dressmaker and wife from Whitehaven; Daniel Kirkbride, 2; Tom Thompson, adopted son, 11; Mary Thompson, mother in law, 55.

51 Scalegill, was occupied by 7 people in 1891: Edward Jeffret, 50, iron miner from Ludgvan Cornwall; Eliza, 50, wife from Ludgvan; with their five children named Edward, 26, iron miner from Ludgvan; Robert, 19, iron miner from Newsome Northumberland; Thomas, 16, iron miner from Frizington; and Mary Ann (11) and Eliza (13).

52 Scalegill, was occupied by 6 people in 1891: George Nicholson, 39, platelayer from Distington; Elizabeth, 45, wife and their four children aged 14 to 5 years old.

53 Scalegill, was occupied by 3 people in 1891: Richard Moyle, 38, iron miner from Stithians Cornwall; Sarah J., 35, wife from Cornwall; Richard (4) from Egremont.

54 Scalegill, was occupied by 3 people in 1891: Robert Grime, 31, iron miner from Hull Yorkshire; Jane, 22, wife from Penzance Cornwall and their infant son Robert born at Egremont.

55 Scalegill, was occupied by 5 people in 1891: Richard Lowery,, iron miner from Egremont; Bessie, 24, wife from Wadebridge Cornwall; their two children and James Swiss, 34, lodger and iron miner from Manchester.

56 Scalegill, was occupied by 6 people in 1891: Robert Bouch, 31, labourer at engine works: Mary A., 26, wife; and their four children aged 8 to infant.

57 Scalegill, was occupied by 3 people in 1891: Henry Trevaskis, 47, iron miner, Mary, 22 wife; and their daughter Elizabeth, 20, a general servant. They all hailed from Ludgvan Cornwall. The ages of Mary and Elizabeth are confirmed to be as shown on the original census record.

58 Scalegill, was occupied by 3 people in 1891: John Readman, 21, locomotive fireman; Alice, 20, wife; Mary J, 1.

59 Scalegill, was occupied by 5 people in 1891: John Willis, 47, iron miner from Wendron Cornwall; Emily, 44, wife, from Camborne Cornwall, and their three children aged 14 to 8 years old.

60 Scalegill, known as 'Bay Horse Inn', was occupied by 7 people in 1891: Robert Wilson, 52, labourer and inn keeper; Catherine, 43, wife; their four children aged 11 to 5; and Isabella Macauley, 18 from Harrington who worked as a servant.

Moor Row in 1891

61 Scalegill, was occupied by 3 people in 1891: John Glanville, 27, iron miner of Cleator; Anne, 26, wife; Isaac Milburn, 23, iron miner and lodger from Askam Lancashire.

62 Scalegill, was occupied by 3 people in 1891: Jane Brocklebank, 60, widow from Nether Wasdale; William, 25, son and iron miner; Joseph, 20, son and iron miner.

63 Scalegill, was occupied by 10 people in 1891: Robert Hitchin, 37, iron miner of Irton; Sarah, 34, wife; and their eight children aged 14 to infant.

Scalegill Road in 1891

1 Scalegill Road, was occupied by 9 people in 1891: Isaac Dixon, 57, iron miner from Kendal; Elizabeth, 49, wife; Mary, 15; John 14; Mark, 11; Annie, 9; William Swandle, grand son, 2; Isaac Dixon Swandle, grand son, infant; and Isaac Kitchin, 64, lodger and general labourer.

In 1871 Isaac and Elizabeth were recorded living at Ingwell View Egremont with their older children Isaac junior, 4; James, 3; and Sarah E., 1. Also William J Twentman was lodging with them. By 1881 the family had moved to Moor Row and grown by three more children.

By 1901 Isaac and Elizabeth were living at 47 Scalegill. Isaac, then 68, was still working as a miner, and their sons John and Mark were labourers in the iron mines. Ann, then 19, worked as a dress maker. Their grand son William F Dixon, then 12, also lived with them.

2 Scalegill Road, was occupied by 7 people in 1891: William Thomas, 41, iron miner from St Just Cornwall; Elizabeth, 38, wife of St Just; William C., 16 from St Just; Gabriel, 13 from St Just; Mary, 8; George H., 6; Emelia, 4.

In 1881 William had been working as a tin miner in St Just, living with Elizabeth and the two oldest children.

Moor Row Residents 1891- Organised By Streets.

3 Scalegill Road, was occupied by 3 people in 1891: James Troon, 31, iron miner from Ludgvan Cornwall; Elizabeth, 26, wife; John James, aged 1.

4 Scalegill Road, was occupied by 5 people in 1891: George Watson, 55 railway platelayer from Millom; Isabella, 56, wife from Scotland; John, married son, 24, grocers assistant from Egremont; Ethel, 9; Margaret, 25, daughter in law.

5 Scalegill Road, was occupied by 8 people in 1891: William Lavery, 31, railway goods guard from Egremont; Frances, 37, wife; Isaac, 8; Fanny, 9; Sarah A., 7; James, 5; Robert, 3; Harold, 1.

6 Scalegill Road, was occupied by 10 people in 1891: James Stopard, 46, foreman at railway carriage works form Lupton Derbyshire; Harriet, 43, wife from Lupton; Eva A., 23, school teacher from Lupton; Bertha, 20, milliner from Lupton; William J., 17, railway clerk from Darnall Yorkshire; Janet M., 16 from Darnall; Emily, 11 from Barrow in Furness; Ada, 9 from Barrow; Albert A., 7; Samuel G., 4 from Egremont.

> James and Harriet were living at New Tupton Chesterfield, Derbyshire in 1871. In 1881 James worked as a railway wagon builder, living with Harriet, and their children Eva, Frederick, and Bertha, at 14 Dumfries Street Barrow.

> By 1901 James and Harriet were living at 147 Greengate Street Barrow where James worked as a foreman in the Barrow carriage works. Also, Janet, then 26, working as a dress maker; with Ada; Albert A., working as an insurance clerk; Samuel G., then 14 and working as an office boy in the ship yard. By 1911 James, Harriet, Albert and Samuel lived at 21 Roose Road Barrow.

7 Scalegill Road, was occupied by 2 people in 1891: James Singers, 66 railway traffic inspector from Ireland; Eliza, 64, wife from Leeds Yorkshire.

8 Scalegill Road, was occupied by 9 people in 1891: Stephen Nicholls, 38, iron miner of Ludgvan Cornwall; Hannah B., 37, wife from Egremont; William J., son, 16, an engine fitter from Egremont; Mary, 15; Elizabeth, 13 Stephen 11; Richard, 7; Hannah, 6; George H., 4; all of Frizington.

9 Scalegill Road, was occupied by 4 people in 1891: Robert Wilkinson, 39, mine overman from Gainsborough Lincolnshire; Bridget, 34, wife from Hensingham; Edith, 6; Emily, 4.

Robert and Bridget had lived at Moor Row in 1881. They had moved to 24 Scalegill Road with their daughters by 1901, then to 26 Scalegill Road by 1911. In 1911 Edith was an elementary school teacher and Emily worked as a dressmaker.

10 Scalegill Road, was occupied by 3 people in 1891: William Muncaster, 67, retired iron miner from Beckermet; Elizabeth, 61, wife from Muncaster; Mary E., daughter aged 17.

11 Scalegill Road, was occupied by 8 people in 1891: William Nicholson, 56. tailor of Gosforth; Ann, 43, wife; Wilson Nicholson, son 22, tailor from Santon; Rhoda, 19; Ruth H., 16; Annie, 10; Alfred; 3. Also Anthony Murray, lodger and tailors apprentice.

12 Scalegill Road, was occupied by 5 people in 1891: William T James, 31, clerk to ore mine; Mary, 27, wife; Sarah E., 6; Ethel, 5: Christopher, 3.

13 Scalegill Road, was occupied by 7 people in 1891: Joseph Mawson, 37, iron miner from Millom; Abigail, 34, wife from Whitehaven; Ann, 11; Mary, 10; Alexander, 8; William, 6; and Abigail, 1 year old.

14 Scalegill Road, was occupied by 2 people in 1891: Ann Fee, widow of 59, grocer from Douglas Isle of Man; Elizabeth, Ann's daughter, 19. grocers assistant. Ann's house doubled as the grocery.

Moor Row Residents 1891- Organised By Streets.

15 Scalegill Road, was occupied by 5 people in 1891: Joseph Nicholson, 40, iron miner of Irton; Mary Ann, 34, wife; George D., 9; Edward, 7; Elizabeth, 4.

16 Scalegill Road, was occupied by 9 people in 1891: Peter Hand, 43, iron miner from Ludgvan Cornwall; Elizabeth, 45, wife from Ludgvan; William Hand, son, 17, iron miner; Peter, 15; Jane; 11; Mary E., 10; Samuel, 9; Richard, 7; Alma, 2- all born Egremont.

17 Scalegill Road, was occupied by 4 people in 1891: John Hodgson, 29, iron miner; Jane A., 28, wife; Margaret E., aged 1; and James, infant.

18 Scalegill Road, was occupied by 3 people in 1891: Emily Roberts, 41, married; Amelia B., 15, school teacher from St Levan; William Wilson, 25, lodger and iron miner from Cumberland. In 1881 Emily and Amelia were living with her parents John (62, a carpenter) and Amelia Chapple (63, and described as 'tin miners wife'), at Trebehor Cottage in St Levan.

19 Scalegill Road, was occupied by 5 people in 1891: Thomas Mitchell, 40, iron miner from St Ives Cornwall; Ellen, 38, wife from Bierton Cornwall; William, 15; Emma J., 14; Anne D., 12. The children were born in Egremont. They also had a son Thomas, born 1881, who is not listed with them in 1891.

20 Scalegill Road, was occupied by 4 people in 1891: William Shaw, 32, iron miner from Hensingham; Jessie, 30, wife; Thomas H., 2; Margaret Shaw from Hensingham, widow and mother.

21 Scalegill Road, was occupied by 6 people in 1891: John Fee, 31, blacksmith; Mary Ann May, 34, wife; James, 9; William, 7; Joseph, 6; Ann, 3.

22 Scalegill Road, was occupied by 3 people in 1891: Thomas Davey, 45, iron miner of Gulval Cornwall; Mary, 46, wife from Ireland; Margaret, 8 born Ireland.

23 Scalegill Road, was occupied by 5 people in 1891: John Poole, 40, locomotive driver from Dalton Lancashire; Mary Ann, 37, wife from Leyton Lancashire; Hannah, 17; John W., 9; Mary A., 2; all born Barrow in Furness.

24 Scalegill Road, was occupied by 6 people in 1891: William Watson, 41, iron miner of Barrow in Furness; Jane, 44, wife from Lancashire; Walton B Haile, stepson, 17, iron mine labourer from Egremont; Mary Watson, 12; Jennie G., 10; Thomas Haile, nephew, locomotive driver.

In 1881 William, Jane and the children had been living at 25 Summerhill Bigrigg. In 1901 William and Jane were running a guest house at Sella Bank Seascale.

25 Scalegill Road, was occupied by 7 people in 1891: James Berryman, 41, iron miner of Cornwall; Ellen, 43, wife from Cornwall; James junior, 16 from Cornwall; John, 14; Richard, 9; Benjamin, 7; Farah E., 5.

26 Scalegill Road, was occupied by 6 people in 1891: Jane Doloughan, 52, married and living on own means from Haydon Bridge Northumberland; Henry, 19, quarryman, Annie, 17, dress maker; Lizzie, 15; Jane, 13; John, 11. On the day the census was recorded there were also three visitors staying- Mathew Gribble, 42 railway station master; Mary Gribble, 36, wife; William H., 11.

> In 1881 Jane was living at Jacktrees Farm with her husband John Doloughan from Ireland. They were proprietors of 80 acres of land helped by three men. Joshua Robson, 18, their nephew, from Whitfield Northumberland also lived with them. Joshua worked as a clerk.
>
> By 1901 Jane, Lizzie and John were living together at 26 Scalegill Road. Lizzie was a dress maker and John was a mechanical engineers apprentice.

27 Scalegill Road, was occupied by 11 people in 1891: Thomas Barnes,

54, iron miner from Coniston; Elizabeth, 49, wife from Isle of Man; Thomas, 26, son, iron miner from Egremont; John, 20, iron miner; William, 18, iron miner; Joseph, 16; Ann, 13; Samuel, 12; Jane, 10; Elizabeth, 8. Also, Elizabeth A Williams, 17, domestic servant from Egremont.

28 Scalegill Road, was occupied by 4 people in 1891: Elizabeth Hodgson, 56, widow of Gosforth; William, son, 21 iron miner of Egremont; James, son, 19 iron miner of Egremont; William Wilkinson, 33, widower and railway labourer of Cartmel Lancashire.

29 Scalegill Road, was occupied by 4 people in 1891: Maragaert A Shaw, 33; Thomas, 13; James, 10; John, 9.

30 Scalegill Road, was occupied by 4 people in 1891: Ann Smith, 65, widow; Joseph Elliott, lodger, 25 and grocer, Eleanor Elliott, lodger, married, 21; Elizabeth Elliott, infant.

31 Scalegill Road, was occupied by 4 people in 1891: John Ashbridge, 69, joiner; Margaret, 55, wife; 'E H', infant daughter; Thomas Ashbridge, 93, widower and retired iron miner.

32 Scalegill Road, was occupied by 5 people in 1891: James Simpson, 41, iron miner; Esther, 44, wife; Henrietta, 13; Frances, 11; David Wrightson, lodger, 60, widower and platelayer from Durham.

33 Scalegill Road, was occupied by 7 people in 1891: John Hogg, 44, blacksmith from Carlisle; Martha, 46, wife; Sarah, daughter, 21; James F., 17 blacksmith; Thomas, 15, mineral borer in mine; Martha, 10; John, 2.

School Street Moor Row in 1891

1 School Street was occupied by 5 people in 1891: George Bowness, 29, iron miner of Egremont; Jane, 25, wife; Elizabeth A., 7; Thomas, 5; John, 2.

Also recorded in the census were the Moor Row Board School and the Wesleyan Chapel with Sunday School.

Station Terrace Moor Row in 1891

1 Station Terrace was occupied by 4 people in 1891: John Murdock, 60, locomotive driver of Durham; Isabella, wife, 59, of Parton; Thomas, 18. railway accountant; Alfred, 16, coachman.

2 Station Terrace was occupied by 5 people in 1891: Hugh Fraser, 33, railway signalman of Wickam Durham; Hannah L., 34, wife of Cumberland; George, 6' Margaret L., 4; Clara C., aged 1.

3 Station Terrace was occupied by 8 people in 1891: William Linfoot, 29, railway signalman of Yorkshire; Annie, 30, wife from Lamplugh; John 6; Alice, 4; Elizabeth, 2; Mark, infant. Also John Thompson, 22, lodger and platelayer of Egremont; John Wilkinson, 20, lodger and railway clerk of Whitehaven.

4 Station Terrace was occupied by 5 people in 1891: Thomas Bird, 40, railway wagon builder from Staffordshire; Susannah, 38, wife of Oldbury; William Bird, son, 20, wagon builder; Thomas Bird, son, 18 locomotive stoker, Mary Bird, 13; all of Oldbury.

5 Station Terrace was occupied by 4 people in 1891: Susan Hannay, 47, widow from Liverpool; Isabella F., daughter, 24, school caretaker from Egremont; Thomas H. Hannay, son 21, railway clerk; John F P Hannay, 18, railway clerk.

6 Station Terrace was occupied by 10 people in 1891: William Richardson, 38, locomotive driver; Mary, 36, wife; Hannah, 17; Thomas, 16 railway porter; Eliza, 10; Mary J., 9; Margaret, 7; Robert, 3; William, 1; Maria Eilbeck, widow, 81.

7 Station Terrace was occupied by 3 people in 1891: Henry Stewart, railway platelayer from Gosforth; Fanny, 30, wife; Harry Stewart, 2.

Moor Row Residents 1891- Organised By Streets.

8 Station Terrace was occupied by 5 people in 1891: Henry Mossop, 42, railway passenger guard; Mary, 44, wife; Mary J., 15; Isaac, 12; Laura E., 5.

In 1881 Henry and Mary had lived at 'Concreet Roe' Egremont with Mary J. and Isaac. They had another daughter Josephine, born 1898.

In 1901 Isaac was working as a railway passenger guard. By 1911 Isaac had married Hannah (born 1882) and they lived at 27 Penzance Street with their daughter Marion Dixon Mossop, 6, and Henry Watson Mossop, 3. They also had two boarders, John Doggart, 25, ore mine labourer; and Thomas Reese, 34, ore mine labourer.

9 Station Terrace was occupied by 5 people in 1891: William Wilcock, 46, railway passenger guard from Holme Westmorland; Mary, 48, wife from Arlecdon; Sarah R Smith, 15, stepdaughter and teacher from Liverpool; Mary E Wilcock, 14, dress maker of Egremont; William Wilcock, son, 11.

10 Station Terrace was occupied by 7 people in 1891: Henry Richardson, 57, railway traffic inspector from Workington; Sarah, wife, 45 from Whitehaven; Cindinia J., daughter, dress makers apprentice; Ada S., 14; William H., 10; Thomas P., 7; George A., 5.

In 1871 ad 1881 Henry and Sarah had been living at Gutterby with their daughters Margaret A (born 1867)., Mary J. (born 1870), and Catherine H., (born 1873) as well as Lindania (sic), Ada, and William.

By 1901 Henry and Sarah still lived at 10 Station Terrace which was occupied then by 9 people: Margaret A Briggs (daughter), dressmaker; Catherine H Richardson (daughter); Sindanies I Richardson (daughter and dress maker) with her husband Thomas P Richardson (railway porter); George A., farm labourer; Robenee Briggs,, grand daughter born 1890; and Catherine Partington, born 1823, widow

The Destitute Paupers of the Parish.

Notably absent from the census are unemployed residents. Under Poor Law rules, property owners paid a tax to look after people living in poverty by building hostels called Work Houses where they lived. They did compulsory work to contribute to their keep. Amongst the paupers were sick, disabled, deserted, broken, and unemployed people and their families. Work houses had the reputation for cruelty, and many people took to wandering in search of casual work. They were called variously tramps, beggars, vagrants, or potters,[26] described by Dorothy Wordsworth as the victims of society.

The Potters

In winter there was a potters camp at Wigton Cumberland, amongst others, and in summer the potters took to tramping again. The Keswick constable counted 42,000 potters on the roads around Bassenthwaite during the hard times of 1848, looking for work and living on the road side. Tourists to the Lake District were greatly outnumbered by the destitute looking for work, immortalised in William Wordsworth's 'Beggars' poem as '…a matriarchal society of Amazonian women and useless drones for menfolk' [Marshall, 1971, pp 119 – 127].

---

[26] Called 'Potters', on account of them making a living by selling earthenware door to door. They were also known for selling brooms, fire wood, baskets and beehives, as well as taking labouring work when available.

Chapter 6

LIVING MEMORIES OF MOOR ROW IN 2021

In 2021 Moor Row had a pie and cake shop on Scalegill Road. It closed that year after the COVID worldwide outbreak of 2020 meant that people meeting up or going outdoors was greatly restricted by the United Kingdom government. There was a Post Office on Church Street that closed a few years earlier. There have been many other shops in the village over the years. An article in the Whitehaven News written by Stanley and Marjorie Young talked about Village Life in the thirties in Moor Row. Stanley recalled "There were so many shops in Moor Row in the 30s you hardly had to go anywhere else. There was Jack Lancaster's joiners and undertaker, Ernie Williams painter and decorator, Eddie Nicholson's plumbers, the post office, Totty Horn's barbers shop, Maggie Johnson's off-licence, Albert Nichol the clogger, the Co-op store, two shops on Dalzell Street and 2 fish and chip shops. There was a confectioners and bakers, two coal agents and two women selling wet fish from a horse and cart."

The article was discussed on internet social media and provoked recollections by other residents who identified other shops and services that could be added to the list.

Here are some of the answers from 2020

'I think Doctor Richie was the first to have the surgery on Church Street'

'Folks used to buy fresh hot newly baked bread etc from my fathers van, J&J Murrays Egremont, on our back street .'My nanna and granda had a shop on Dalzell St'.

'My grandad Marra, used to sell his garden produce lettuce etc he would walk up from Wall House to Moor Row, he also had eggs from his bantams'

'The old man over the road lived there all his life, and said he remembered 75 Penzance street as a toy shop. When we took the dash off out the front of the house we could see in the brickwork where an old sign used to be'

'Low Farm milk, collect or delivered, and in season vegetables plus roundsmen providing meat fish fruit confectionery not forgetting 'Keks' at Scalegill for the best cooked meats'

'Chip shop was 5 or 6 houses up from the Pub, Station, One shop was 4 or 5 doors below opening on the other side (Mrs Wilsons in my day)'.

What about Alec O'Neil with his fruit cart he used to stable his horse at wood end

'My nannas shop was at no 51 I think. I remember her having a big selection of halfpenny/penny sweets on counter. Think it was just like a convenience store. When they left it they moved to no 52.'

'There was also Jock Jenkinson and Walter who delivered coal.'

'What about William Alan Graham he had a coal business he lived on dalzell st he had a horse and cart'

'There was a milliners where the doctor's surgery used to be I was told.'

'Nickels then the Downs family. Harry, Mary and sons Ray and Roger.

Spent many an afternoon there. Harry Downs took all the boys in the village on Saturday rambles to the lakes and the local beaches. Great days.'

'Martha's, Mrs Wilson's dalzell st, post office, Mrs drakes, Elsie horns, coop, Ernie Williams wallpaper shop grandmas kekks that's all I remember undertaker, chip shop'.

'1 shop…Keck's….1 pub Jack and Mable Thompson…1 Farm Benny Pennington'

'Matha's sweet shop on Penzance Steet and her penny tray.'

'Our house use to be a wall paper shop. An mrs Cowen told me years ago hers was a post office one time.'

Mr Williams (or Williamson) had the wall

paper shop on the corner of Scalegill Road and Mr and Mrs Bone the Post Office on the cross roads. Just further along next to the Coop was Totty Horn the hairdresser who scalped all the lads but had Vimto in bottles.'

'Ernie William's his wife was school teacher at moor row school. it was number 1 scalegill Road.'

'It was 2 doors up from where the post office was. Next to the Post Office was where John Eilbeck lived, then the grocer's shop belonging to Mabel Drake and then Dorothy Taylor then there was Elsie's. She was mainly sold sweets, lemonade, crisps and more.'

'Don't forget Annie millers fish and chips on dalzell St she also sold ice lollies. From her house 76 penzance St.'

'Any remember Mollie Wilson's shop ?'

'Emma Goodwyn also had the fish and chip shop at the bottom of Dalzell St.'

Moor Row in 1891

'So did Annie Miller'

'Fish and chip shop called Cardwells next door to you.'

'My mam got knitting wool at mrs Wilton's then olive davys.'

'I used to get my hair cut at Totti's. Only one style available but it lasted for ages. Got a bottle of Vimto while waiting. Went for bread in grocer shop next door. If "stinky Newton" came in everyone else cleared out.

'I was told the houses with big windows in Dalzell Street Moor Row were shops, but there are more shops listed above than big windows in the street. Ours was supposed to be a bakers shop, with a small window, and then there were sweet shops, cobblers, barber, coal man, co-op, and more. Never heard of a chip shop though!'

'Annie miller was also the post lady in moor row for years'

'The name Goodwin, I think, wet fish '.

'We have people visit who remember getting their wedding cake made by the previous resident. She was a confectioner.'

Chapter 7

MOOR ROW IN GOVERNMENT RECORDS

During the 1800s the English government found it necessary to keep records of what people were up to. They started a simple register of people in 1801, to see how many people might be conscripted to fight wars in Europe against Emperor Napoleon. After that first register, the census of 1801, the government thought of a few more reasons why counting up people might help them. Over the 220 years of keeping records the list of government interests has grown, to measure things like:

- Ability of the government to fight wars.
- Planning food production.
- Stimulating life insurance company business.
- The amount of sick and infirm workers in the country .
- House sizes and occupancy in workers houses.
- Distribution of types of work.
- Amenities in private housing.
- Peoples qualifications.
- Amount of car ownership.
- Ethnicity and immigrant status.
- Military service history.
- Gender identity.

Keeping these records showed there were problems in recording even basic stuff, like actually defining an address where some one lived, as parishes shifted boundaries to divert their responsibilities and also attract greater benefits.[27] The uncertainties with boundaries were eventually sorted so that reliable and unique addresses became available for reliable data recording and rational resource allocation.

Moor Row has been given a few names over the years, on maps and in government records, like Moorow, Ingwell View, Gutterby, Scalegill, and Low Keekle. In 1829 three homesteads in the area were named as Low Moorrow, High Moorrow, and a second High Moorow Farm.[28] The Ordnance Survey maps in 1860 named Moor Row as Low Keekle and the railway station as Moor Row Junction, but by 1891 the name 'Moor Row' was established on Ordnance Survey maps and the government census.

In 1891, the UK Census recorded almost 30 million people living in England and Wales, 5 million living in all Ireland, and 4 million in Scotland. The 30 million people of England and Wales lived in roughly five and a half million households- between 5 and 6 people on average in each household. 11% of households were designated as overcrowded, that is more than 2 people per occupied room (kitchen, bedrooms, living rooms). Overcrowding was more common in urban areas (almost 13% of households in town urban areas, and almost 9% in country rural areas were designated overcrowded), and over crowding was more common in smaller houses.

Overcrowding affected 13% of the population in Cumberland, over 30% in Northumberand and Durham, and 3% in England's garden of Kent. Sunderland, London, and Newcastle had the highest average occupancy of 7 people per household.

In 1891 about half the people of Britain lived in towns and the other half lived in the countryside. By 1891 the population density for England

---

[27] Philip Kitchen is listed living at Scalegill Hall in St Bees, yet the homesteads called Moor Row and Shaw were sometimes listed in Egremont.
[28] Parson and White, 1829, p208.

and Wales had increased throughout the century. It was calculated that if everyone was stood the same distance apart throughout England and Wales, they would all be 85 yards apart, the same as 78 meters apart or the width of Manchester City's football pitch. At that rate everyone would get one half of the Etihad stadium pitch each,[29] if the country was shared equally.

In 2021 the population of England and Wales was almost 60 million in 24 million households. 10 million of them lived in London. If all the land were shared equally there would be 600 people per square mile (370 per square kilometre) or one third of a football pitch each. There are 60 million acres of land in the UK, 30 million being England and 5 million in Wales so plenty to go round. Over half of that land is owned by just 1 person in every hundred who lives here, and the other 99 people are living on the other half. That is an average 5 acres for just a few people and an average half an acre for 60 the million of the rest.

The 24th biggest land owner is Hugh Lowther, Earl of Lonsdale who owns 35,000 acres, as does James Dyson who makes vacuum cleaners. The King and his family own about 1,000,000 (a million) acres in 2020, about the same as the British army, while the Forestry Commission own 2 million acres.[30]

In 1861 Moor Row and Scalegill had grown to 200 people living in the 38 new houses built since the railway arrived. That's about five people in each household. By 1891 there were 291 households with 1203 residents, living in Fishers Court, Gutterby, Scalegill, Church Street, Dalzell Street, John Street, Penzance Street, Scalegill Road, Railway Terrace, School Street, Station Terrace, the three homesteads known as 'Moor Row', 'Low Moor Row' and 'High Moor Row', and the larger houses known as Victoria Villas and Alva House. The census for Moor Row showed there were about four people living together in each household, with some houses being home for eleven people.

---

[29] Or Old Trafford, etc.
[30] www.abcfinance.co.uk/blog/who-owns-the-uk

Crowded housing was not always forced on people. In the agricultural homesteads the proprietors used people for the heavy business of working the land for them. In the genteel houses, the owners took advantage of cheap workers to do the menial work for them, like fetching coal, cleaning house, and cooking. In 1871 Jonas Lindow (born 1848) and his sister Eliza lived at Ehen Hall with their mother Ann Eliza and father John. They needed 6 servants and a nurse to look after them. In 1881 Jonas lived with his mother and sister, still at Ehen hall, and they had 8 servants to take care of them. By 1891 Jonas and his sister had cut back to 7 servants, a butler, a maid, a cook, 2 housemaids, 1 kitchen maid and 1 laundry maid. In 1901 Jonas was living at Ingwell where he was described as 'Proprietor of iron mines, Justice of the Peace, and Deputy Lieutenant of Cumberland'. He had 11 servants to look after himself, his three female cousins and Mary Proctor who was visiting from Ireland.

In 1891, Jonas Lindow Burns-Lindow living at Irton Hall with his wife, and their 6 children were looked after by their 13 house servants. This Jonas died in 1893 from a throat infection called 'quinsy'. Tyson Herbert lived at Scalegill Hall with his wife, 6 children and his 81 year old grand mother Jane Tyson: They had two servants to look after them. Meanwhile at Montreal Farm Thomas Pearson lived with his 78 year old mother Eleanor, his sister Bridget and 3 servants to look after them. Pearson's near neighbour, William Threlfell of Low Hall Thurnham, St Bees, had 3 house servants to look after his house hold of 11 people.

As well as over crowding, the census of 1891 was concerned with gathering data on people excluded from working. So, a record was kept of how many people were suffering the 'grave infirmities' of blindness, deafness and dumbness together, idiocy, imbecility and lunacy. No one was recorded with such illnesses in Moor Row in 1891. Throughout the United Kingdom in 1891 about 1 in 600 were classed as idiots, imbeciles or lunatics; about 1 in 1000 were blind; and 1 in 2000 were both deaf and dumb together.

Chapter 8

MAKING MONEY BY MAKING IRON

To make steel, first make some iron. To make iron needs limestone dug from quarries, coal and iron stone dug from the ground, a factory to purify the iron and steel, and a way of hauling all the stuff around, from mines and quarries to furnaces, and from furnaces to people who buy the steel. To make 500 kg of iron takes 500kg of coke and 1500kg of iron ore. To make the 500kg of coke needs 800kg of coal. It takes 8 tons of coal with 4 tons of iron ore and 1 ton of limestone to make 1 ton of steel. A car is made from about one ton of steel, and 100 million cars are made each year. Two thousand million tons of steel were made in 2021.

Understanding how to make iron came to Britain from the middle east in around 450 BC, over two thousand years ago. It was first made on an open forge, until mass production methods were developed using tall furnaces that had air blown through them.

- The ingredients to make iron are limestone, ironstone, coke and air. Coke is burned to start the iron purification, ironstone, or iron ore, provides the iron, air is blown through to keep the coke burning, and the limestone soaks up impurities to leave clean iron in the furnace. This mixture of limestone and impurities is called slag. The furnace is operated at about 1200°c and looks white hot when full, hot enough for the iron, limestone and slag to be a liquid that runs like water.

- The molten iron and slag are drained separately from the furnace. Slag is thrown away and iron is drained in to a grid of moulds to cool and set. This is called pig iron, because the arrangement of the moulds was said to resemble a mother pig with feeding piglets. Pig iron is used to make steel, a purer version of iron that is tougher and more durable than brittle pig iron.

Steel is much more use than brittle iron, especially for making tools, cutlery and weapons, but also for ships, cars, beams, engines and much more.

- Steel is made by melting the pig iron and blowing air through it to remove all impurities. A little carbon is then added to make the steel ductile when it cools.

- Industrial scale making of steel started about 1860, when converters could make five tons of steel in about 15 minutes. Before then it took 24 hours to make five tons of steel. The biggest problem when making steel was getting clean iron, and very few iron mines had ore that produced clean iron.

- Cumberland mines were practically the only ones in Europe that did so until new ways of making steel from dirty iron were invented the ore from Cumberland mines was in great demand and was the most expensive to buy.

The advantage lasted twenty years, to about 1880, during which time the Cumberland mines made fortunes for the owners involved, until the Bessemer conversion process was joined with the Gilchrist conversion process for making steel from dirty ore. By 1910 steel and iron prices were virtually equal in Sweden, Germany, Britain and America and only a preference for British metal within its empire slowed the industry's decline [Robert Allen, 1979, p911]/

Chapter 9

MAKING MONEY WITH LAND

The value of land comes from renting the land out, selling the land, or growing stuff on it to sell. In 1876 Jonas Lindow Burns-Lindow's owned 6,000 acres of land which made him £7000 from rents in that year alone,[31] at a time when coal miners earned about fifty pounds in a year, or nothing if they were sick or injured. The Lindow family from the Old Hall area of Cleator, bought Irton Hall, Ehen Hall and Ingwell Mansion. The Ainsworth family who lived at The Flosh and Harecroft Hall owned about 500 acres of Cumberland. In the late 1800s John Stirling of Parkside House Bigrigg, owned 30,000 acres of Scotland.

The major landowners around West Cumbria were the Wyndham family (called the Lord Leconfield)[32], the Lowther family (called the Lord Lonsdale)[33], the Spedding family and the Curwen family. They rented out land to mine owners or factory owners to build mills, mines, furnaces, and towns on it. The mine owners paid a share of the value of the minerals they dug out of the ground, like coal or iron ore, or lime to the land owner,

---

[31] That's about one million pounds rent each year in 2022 prices, and about £7,000 a year for a working miner at 2022 value.

[32] This man should be addressed as 'My Lord' if we meet him because, as a Baron he is meant to be an honourable man of noble birth.

[33] We should call this man 'My Lord' if we speak to him, and his wife is 'My Lady', because as an Earl, he is meant to be an honourable man of noble birth or rank. In case we should ever meet a Duke, he is to be called 'Your Grace', and the same for an Archbishop. A Royal Duke, like Prince Harry of Sussex, is to be called 'Your Royal Highness'. Miners, railway workers, nurses, house keepers, dress makers, teachers are to be addressed as 'mister' or 'misses'.

called a royalty payment.[34] The smaller plots of land around Moor Row were owned by a small group of families. The Postlethwaite family came from Whitehaven, the Dalzell family from Stockhow Hall, Ainsworths from Preston, the Lindow and Benn families of Cleator, along with Reverend J T O'Neil and the trustees acting for the Birley family, who used to own the old flax mill in Cleator. Sometimes, the landowners simply sold the rights to dig the minerals under the ground, so that five groups of people could be involved in digging- the land owner, the mineral rights owner (these two made the most money with least risk), the mine owner, the mine operator, and the miners (who made the least money at the greatest risk).

There are no stories of any land owner or mineral owner ever going under ground in to the mines. They had made money from their land by having what was underneath it dug up and selling that. From 1872 to 1920 one million tons of iron ore were dug up every year in Cumberland [Lancaster and Wattleworth, Appendix 3, p 161], as well as coal, and limestone, to feed iron and steel furnaces by men paid one pound a week using picks and shovels, barrows and bogies, working by candle light in tunnels full of bad air and liable to flooding.

Within 500 metres of the war memorial in Moor Row are the remains of eleven mine shafts that brought iron ore to the surface, in the fields between the Sea to Sea cycle path, the Quaker Bridge, the Keekle River and St Johns church at Bigrigg:

---

[34] Royalties are the agreement to pay a land owner for what is dug up from beneath their land, are also bought and sold. For instance, land at Crossfield, Cleator was leased for 21 years for the Iron Ore Royalties from Joseph Bowerbank, drug-gist of Cockermouth and others, to Anthony Hill of the Plymouth Iron Works, County of Glamorgan. [Anthony Hill died 2 Aug 1862]. In 1865 the agreement was transferred to Richard Fothergill of Aberdare, Thomas Alers Hankey of Fenchurch Street, City of London and Benjamin Bateman of Gracechurch Street, City of London. In 1868 that agreement was transferred to John Stirling of Montreal Mines, near Whitehaven. In 1863 land at closes 11 and 16-18 [in total 1acre 3 roods 7 perches] were sold to the Whitehaven, Cleator and Egremont Railway for £175, and in 1878 further land sold for building.

- There were three pits sunk on Dalzell land, one in the boggy ground behind Pearson Close, and one each side of the Woodend road. The mines were worked mainly by the Maryport Haematite Iron Company, later named the Maryport Haematite Iron and Steel Company

- A Stirling pit in middle of the Montreal Place estate;

- Two pits named for Sir John Walsh, called 'Old' and 'New'. The land and mineral rights were leased from Sir John Benn Walsh by Samuel and John Lindow, who gave up the pits in 1904. It was then taken over by the Bigrigg Mining Company, then the Workington Iron and Steel Company in 1917, which was taken over by the United Steel Company in 1919. The pits were abandoned in 1939.

- Two Miles Postlethwaite pits, Barker pit, Robin Benn pit, and Frear pit. The Robin Benn pit was operated by the Maryport Hematite Company from 1879, which was a partnership of Scots industrialists, and failed in 1882. The railway serving the pit had been dug up by 1885. There is an old postcard of Moor Row streets in which the engine house chimneys for Sir John and Stirling pits can be seen in the views of Church Street.

There were also pit shafts between Moor Row and Bigrigg, around Woodend, and around Crossfield Road between Cleator Moor and Moor Row. When the mine companies had finished lifting ore the land was handed back to the land owner leaving the holes in the ground and piles of muck and rubbish left over next to unwanted buildings. These old shafts became a convenient dump for disposing of rubbish, shown in aerial photos of old mine heads stuffed with polluting and dangerous rubbish[35] like at Fletcher pit.

---

[35] In the period 2017 the Fletcher pit cap collapsed in to the mine taking the heap of rubbish with it that had been fly tipped on top The shaft was left wide open, and used by more fly tippers when trailers of rubbish were poured down it.

In Cleator Moor the iron ore was so close to the surface at Todholes it was dug out as a quarry, called the 'big hole' when it was working. The heap of spoil that came out was called 'the big hill' by the children who played on it. Until 1850 nearly all the ore was shipped to ironworks in Scotland, Wales, and Northern England, but gradually the ironworks owners took part ownerships in the mines to improve control over the business, and eventually the railways were also owned by the same people. New towns were thrown up to house workers for these businesses, at Barrow, Millom, Askam, Cleator Moor, Frizington, Kirkland and Moor Row.

The money made was generally spent on fine houses and grand living, well away from the smut, filth and fumes of industrial sites. Building a new town became a civilising crusade for the Victorian era, and provided cheap houses for the workers. Starting other businesses like harbours, boats, railways, and mills was divine endorsement of individual wealth, and displays of fine art and furniture, grand tours, being seen in society, dressing in smart clothes, hunting, and building more houses to live in were the credentials of success for the very lucky very few.

Chapter 10

LOWTHER'S LUCK

A lot of West Cumberland was in owned by the main landowners before iron making came to dominate the county so completely. They had been gifted the land in the wills of their families and land enclosure laws, and some had taken over the rights to whatever lay beneath the surface. Never had so few people been given such good fortune to make money out of having people pay to grub about in the muck under their land. The fenced in common land had rights to whatever was beneath the surface, and in the space of a few years many landowners realised they could make more money from the coal and iron buried under the ground than what was growing on top of it.[36] It was digging up and selling coal and iron that made West Cumbria around Moor Row grow from a few scattered homesteads to built up towns and villages, that would house the thousands of people needed to work the mines, furnaces, and railways that would make fortunes for a few families.

The family that owned the most land in the Whitehaven area was the Lowthers. Over many years the family bought Seaton Dearham, Ribton, Distington, Kelton, Arlecdon, Weddicar, St Bees, Hensingham, Frizington, Ennerdale and Rottington so they could make money from the mineral

---

[36] 'The most valuable mineral productions being roofing slate and red haematite- being the richest ore in the UK making the best iron and sent to different parts of the country to improve it with common ores to increase ductility of the finished metal'. Bains (1824).

reserves beneath them. Eventually they owned around 95 manors and 70000 acres of land in Cumbria, as well as farms, houses in London, a hunting lodge in Rutland county with 72 rooms, and two houses they called castles. The largest of these, Lowther Castle at Penrith, had almost 400 rooms.

The Lowther family also had their own railway train and their own orchestra that travelled with them. They were friends of English, Scottish and German Kings, Queens and Kaisers who all used to visit their luxury houses.

The Lowther family, whose most senior member became known as Earl of Lonsdale, started as lawyers taking over pieces of land. They did this by fencing in public waste land and charging rents from tenants for the land they lived on. By carefully lending money on small plots of land they could allow the land owner to run up debts that could not be repaid, and then claim the property instead of demanding payment.

Being lawyers, they knew how to use the courts to take away rights to challenge the changes in landownership. In this way they became lords of the manor of Whitehaven and started selling cloth, beef, salt, coal and herring to Irish and Spanish merchants. They also shipped some of the iron ore found under ground to Scotland and Wales to be made in to iron.

The family displayed single minded pursuit of their personal interests,[37] having a reputation for being grasping and unscrupulous in dealings with people.

---

[37] Writing at the time of the English Civil War, Alice Thornton accused Lowther (1st baronet) of cheating his extended family out of legacies in her parents wills. The Lowther family were described as grasping and unscrupulous in their dealings, and switching sides in the civil war from Royalists to Parliament and back to Royalist, depending on which army was approaching. Lowther certainly abandoned his command of Brougham Castle as the Parliamentary army approached in 1644. [Cited in Osborough, W. N. "Wills that go missing- the quest for the lost will of Christopher Wandesford, Lord Deputy of Ireland" and published in 'Reflections on Law and History' Four Courts Press Dublin 2006 pp.8-16.] Thornton's memoirs were published 150 years after they were written as *The Autobiography of Mrs. Alice Thornton*, of East Newton, Co. York

In 1642 Christopher Lowther was made a baronet[38] for paying for soldiers to be sent to fight Irishmen in Ireland for the British King Charles I. He spent most of his time in London, working in Parliament to promote laws that would improve the prospects of his businesses around Whitehaven, as did many landowners.[39] [40] Those businesses were managed through regular and long letters sent to his managers in Whitehaven. The letters were preserved and published in books, so they can be read to this day.[41] They reveal how business involved planning, scheming, manipulating or bullying people when organising the take over of the area.

There can be no doubt that families who got lucky in business behaved the same as Lowther; protecting their interests and themselves with no obvious concern for the troubles of people around them,[42] including their fellow owners. Since other Cumbrian industrialists lived locally there was little need to write so many letters to their managers about tactics, and consequently there is less information about other landowners in Cumbria to use when studying the history of the area.

---

[38] A Baronet is the lowest rank of nobility, and is a hereditary knight. We would call them 'Sir'. Baronets were created by James 1st to sell to people. If they turned them down they were fined instead, more than the price of buying the baronetcy.

[39] In 1829 the local land owners promoted the building of the first railway between Carlisle and Newcastle to increase the value of their land by opening up the area for industry and trading. Most of the railway's sponsors were members of parliament, and it was them who encouraged parliament to pass the laws necessary to build the railway. They also included in the law that steam engines would not be allowed to be seen from their country houses because that would spoil their view, so the trains near their houses were hauled by horses. [W Tomlinson, 1915, p198].

[40] In 1974 the same thing happened with the Health and Safety at Work etc., Act which made worker safety the employers responsibility. But Members of Parliament excluded domestic servants from safety laws in the workplace, because they employed servants and did not want to be spend money making sure servants were safe at work.

[41] For example, David Hainsworth, (1983) has written about the business letters of Sir John Lowther, 2nd baronet, between 1693 and 1698 with his agents John Gale and William Gilpin.

[42] There is a long list of litigation between companies who shared common interests and concerns, but could not bring themselves co-operate when their individual objectives were maybe at risk: "There is no honour among thieves." Proverbs 21:10-11

Given the scale of money making in West Cumbria during its iron boom the owners parsimony can be surprising. Between about 1800 and 1920, around 60 million tons of iron ore were dug from underneath West Cumbria. In 2022 values that amount would sell for about £40 billion, of which £20 billion profit was kept by company owners, £10 billions was spent in wages and building costs, and £5 billion went to the landowners as royalties.

Chapter 11

TRICKLE DOWN OF MONEY

It is argued by people with plenty of money that rich people spend their money to the benefit of poor people, although it would be hard to explain that to a resident pauper of the Whitehaven Workhouse. The argument claims good things 'trickle down' for the poor in the form of charity and work for the butcher, baker, candle maker and wine seller who all sell their things to the rich man.[43]

It is assumed that these purchases are made at a fair price in the trickle down claim, although it is rich people who decide what is fair. It is worth remembering that, before the Ainsworths, Stirlings, and Lindows built the Cleator Moor iron works, practically everyone who lived in the area worked mainly on the land and lived on homesteads. There are no records of the homesteaders or miners buying landed estates, castles, houses in London or fine clothes with the benefits that trickled down their way. The records of working people are limited to where they lived, what job they had, and how they died, presumably because so very few were marked out in history

---

[43] Trickle Down is a prejudiced idea used in 1896 in a speech by William Jennings Bryan that promoted giving more money to rich people to provide prosperity for those who lived and worked at the top of the economic pyramid, in the belief that prosperity would trickle down to the bottom of the heap and benefit all, rather than all sharing in the work equally [cited in Kazin, Michael (2006) 'A Godly Hero: the life of William Jennings Bryan', New York]. In this way the working class are saved from the depravity of idleness, although the rich are of course excused the moral benefits of being exploited at work [Russell, Bertrand *In Praise of Idleness* (2004)].

by improving a working life beyond what was made available to them. Even in 2022 the number of agricultural labourers is much the same as it was before industrialists and entrepreneurs moved in, suggesting very little has been done to change the wealth of the original population. What is more, they continue to live in the same houses and scratch a living from the same land, except in 2022 they are kept going by large government welfare handouts.[44] The 'trickle down' theory does not explain that outcome.

Arguably Cumberland people got very little from industrialisation, except perhaps by having new churches and school houses built.[45] In 2022 values, allowing for inflation, the charitable donations for hospitals made by the mining and railway owners, for schools, libraries and churches would total about £20 million[46] out of the £40,000 million of sales revenue. In 2022 that's like keeping ten thousand pounds for yourself out of every twenty thousand pounds the business had taken in, and spending just one pound on 'good causes'. To get all the ore out the mine owners would dig underneath buildings, causing some of those buildings they put up to collapse in to the mine workings, like the Montreal School and surrounding streets in Cleator Moor!

Some of the good works that were done might not have been much use either. For instance, Jacktrees hospital was built by mine owners for miners who had been injured and maimed at work. Unfortunately the Jacktrees hospital had just four beds for a workforce of thousands. There were many miners terribly injured and killed at work, yet there were no medical staff registered as working in the hospital. It might seem, looking back, to be a very little thing to take care of some one who was injured in the service of a mine owner. But, in effect, Jacktrees was a field dressing station, a

---

[44] In 2016 the average farm made £2,100 from work and £28,300 from subsidies paid by taxpayers money. The typical cereal farmer lost £9500 from farming' Times of London newspaper, 4/ 8/ 2016.

[45] More money was spent on more buildings in Cumberland by the Scotsman Andrew Carnegie who gave away the equivalent of £150 billion to build schools and libraries around the world, made from his American steel business.

[46] Barber, R. 1976; p42.

quiet place for people who had been smashed and broken at work, to lie in while they tried to heal themselves or die.[47] Likewise, paying toward building a school sounds good, until the mine owner digs underneath it and the building sinks in to the ground. There is the claim that the mines provided work for locals, but the workers were brought in to Cumberland from Ireland, Cornwall, and even Russia. And although they provided housing for workers, families could stay only so long as they paid the rent and didn't fall sick, and didn't get injured. There were plenty who did get sick, plenty were injured, and far too many were killed.

In 1827 John Piele, iron ore agent and mine owner,[48] complained about Irish miners being a danger, when he wrote to Lord Londonderry's Durham pits agent John Buddle.[49] He said they were tramps who would only work in a mine when no other work was available. But in 1844 the Lords Lonsdale and Londonderry wanted cheap Irish black leg labour to break miners striking for proper pay. Then they thought 'tramps, Irish, and agricultural labourers would do nicely'[50] leading a Parliamentary commission to report 'six weeks is enough to make a good miner regardless of how little skill they may have at the start'. A work man's life was cheap.

In 1896 mine owner Miles Postlethwaite organised the presentation of a gold clock to his mine manager John Dixon Kendal who was leaving Foxhouses Road in Whitehaven to expand his engineering and mine agency business in London. The clock, from the miners in the Postlethwaites Mines, was an expression of their gratitude for his concerns for their safety.[51]

The mine, still under Kendal s watchful eye a few years later, was described by an inspector as beastly and suffocating with not enough air to keep a

---

[47] J D Marshall (1978) p170.
[48] Of Walker & Peile, engineers from Moresby.
[49] R. Colls: 1987, p13.
[50] Colls, 1987, pp295 – 301. Cooter, R J 2005, pp126 – 135. Parliamentary papers, 1844 (592), 16, p137.
[51] *Whitehaven News*, 16/ 4/ 1896. 'He had always made the safety of the men his greatest study'.

candle flame lit.[52] [53]

In 1898, when the mine head gear caught fire at Postlethwaites mine, it was extinguished to save the mine and miners still underground, not by any brigade of firemen but by the miners themselves. Many were laid off after the fire. When safety of the miners at Postlethwaites was questioned with the English government Winston Churchill[54] himself said safety was quite adequate, and no locals had complained about incompetent managers. Besides, Churchill added, English law did not require checks to be made on iron mine managers competence [55] [56] Four months later three men were blown up in the mine. Within a couple more years Joseph Braithwaite Wilson died from a broken neck after falling in to an ore truck, aged 50. By then the mine was run by Miles' solicitors, the owner having died from small pox in Mombasa while on a world tour holiday, aged 41.

Around Moor Row the following lives were wrecked while working for owners profits that had 'trickled up' just as the workers luck 'trickled out'.

In the Postlethwaite Mines the following should be remembered for their suffering:

- James Clarkson died from gangrene in the Whitehaven Pauper House, caused by a foot injury, aged 71.

- James Fisher died one month after having his legs broken and head injured after a rock fall.

- Bob Maxwell was killed in a rock fall, aged 32. His family had come from Ireland to improve their security through work.

- John Fletcher, of Moor Row, had his thigh broken, but was at least

---

[52] ibid 21/ 7/ 1898.
[53] Ibid, 1/ 8/ 1889, Mines Act Prosecution At Moor Row.
[54] In those days Churchill was Home Secretary, when he introduced laws to improve coal mine safety and shop workers conditions.
[55] ibid, 1/ 07/ 1911.
[56] Hansard HC Deb 19 June 1911 vol 27 cc16-7

carried home from work to recover.

- Cornelius Sloan was taken home to Cleator Moor on a cart by the Moor Row homesteader Henry Hartley to recover from his broken right leg.
- Willy Reid got carted home by Henry Hartley to the Distressed Sailor to recover from head injuries and a broken collar bone caused by a pick axe falling down the mine shaft.
- Mr. A. Byers was concussed and had a deep head wound from a rockfall.
- George Bell had his broken shoulder blade treated at home, after Henry Hartley carted him there, caused by being dragged along a tunnel by a mine truck.
- John Sewel was blinded by an underground explosion, in which Edward Crear from Scalegill injured his arm, and John Tynan's head was injured.

In the Fletcher Pits, the following should be remembered:

- Edward Young, aged 17, killed by a rock fall.
- Edward Telfer aged 28, killed by a rail wagon falling down the shaft from the surface.
- In 1869 the owners of Fletcher Pit, who were trustees for the field owner, the late Isabella Fletcher, found time to instruct solicitors to claim for mismanagement of the mine that reduced their profits. The people who worked the mine, the executors of the will of the late Welsh iron factory owner Anthony Hill also paid solicitors to defend the claim. The trustees won £6,500, worth a million pounds in 2022. The mine carried on working throughout the case. The solicitor for the trustees was John Postlethwaite, of Hollins

house. Miles Postlethwaite who also lived at Hollins went on to own the Postlethwaite mines at Eskett and Moor Row.

In the Sir John Walsh Pits, the following lives were destroyed:

- Albert Moore Aston, aged 33, died from head injures a year after being hit on the head underground by a roof fall. The mine owners tried to claim the brain tumour was not the fault of the bang to his head which ruined his previous good health. Poor Albert's brain was showed at the inquest in Cleator Moor, having been kept illegally after his funeral had taken place! The local Labour M.P. Thomas Gavan Duffy helped win a claim for £300 compensation for Albert's widow, equivalent to £6,000 in 2022.

- Thomas Henry Bell, aged 34, died three weeks after breaking his leg when jumping clear of a falling mine roof, which had also caused blood poisoning.

- John Connors of Aldby Street Cleator Moor, was killed by a runaway bogey.

- Thomas Cowen of Keekle Terrace, died after being caught by a rock fall, aged 46.

- John Cromwell, aged 20, of Cleator Moor, died in Whitehaven Infirmary after a seven ton rock fell and crushed his left leg and hand.

- Richard Hocking aged 57, of Montreal Street Cleator Moor killed by a rock fall, in 1937.

- George Juke, aged 54, killed by rock fall.

- William Mitchell, aged 36, of Croft Terrace Egremont died in Whitehaven Infirmary form head and feet injuries after a mine accident.

- Wilfred Norman was killed by moving machinery crushing his head.

- John William Southam, aged 26, killed in 280 metre fall down the shaft after a working platform was removed. The coroner decided that no particular safety fencing was required when the pit shaft was left open so people could work around it.

- James Southward of Springfield Road Bigrigg died in Whitehaven Infirmary from head injuries, a day after being hit by a roof fall. James was married, aged 22.

- Joseph Sparks, 63, of Trumpet Terrace died at Whitehaven Infirmary a day after being crushed below the waist by a rock fall. Mr Gavan Duffy complained at the inquest that miners expenses were not being paid to help the inquest collect evidence.

- Robert Wilkinson of Penzance Street Moor Row killed by blood poisoning three weeks after a rock fall had crushed his leg and stripped all its skin off, requiring the leg to be amputated two weeks after the injury. Robert had been taken home first before being transferred to the Infirmary.

The Sir John Walsh pits were originally worked by the Lindows of Cleator, with about 25 people. From 1910 the United Steel Company, later called the Workington Iron and Steel Company Ltd employed about 220 people before selling out to the Bigrigg Mining Company Ltd.

There were two mines within Moor Row, under land once owned by two of the Dalzell family called Thomas Henry and John. They had both died by 1875. Five people are recorded as having died in these mines.

- Mark Daniels, aged 29, killed by dynamite explosion.

- Edward Ennis of Dalzell Street Moor Row, aged 61, died from heart failure while mining.

- Matthew Johnson, aged 50, of Scalegill, killed instantly by roof collapse.[57]

---

[57] Sometimes referred to as 'Parliament Pit'.

- Felix Lee, aged 40. Died three days after a pit cage fell down the shaft on to him.

- Benjamin Mitchell, aged 55, of Moor Row, killed instantly by a roof fall in 1870.

- Joseph Pearson killed by a machine malfunction.

- In 1878 John Madden, 27, from Moor Row, had his legs crushed by a roof fall. His left foot was mutilated, and his right leg so badly injured it was held on with just strips of skin. The leg was cut off using scissors.

- In 1880 Thomas Maguire of Cleator Moor had his hand blown off during blasting work.

- In 1884 James Burns of Aldby Street Cleator Moor had a leg broken by a rock fall.

The rights to mine where let out by Dalzell trustees and executors to a number of different companies over the space of 30 years. The two mines are called the Moor Row (Iron Ore) mine held by the executors of Thomas Henry Dalzell, and Dalzell Moor Row Iron Ore Mine, held by trustees of John Dalzell of Hayton (died 1875) respectively. The Moor Row (Iron Ore) Mine, on Thomas Henry's former land, was operated variously by the Lindow brothers Samuel and John, The Moor Row Mining Company, and The Crossfield Iron Ore Company. The Dalzell Moor Row Iron Ore Mine, which was John's, was operated variously by John Stirling, the Maryport Haematire Iron and Steel Company, the Walker and Piele Company, and by Brown, Burnyeat and Company. John Piele was agent for the Lonsdale Whitehaven mines in 1827, and was instrumental in recruiting miners to Cumberland. The two mines employed about forty people. They worked between 1894 to 1913 and raised about 7,000 tons of ore a year between them. They were left to flood in 1926.

'My Lord' the Baron Leconfield of Petworth House had mines at Bigrigg, in which at least 11 miners were killed.

- Daniel Dawson, was tipped from cage down the shaft, aged 27.
- Joseph Haige, was crushed, aged 32.
- John McGinns, crushed, a widower who left six children unprovided for.
- William Mossop, was crushed, aged 32, left a widow and two children.
- Nicholas Griffin, aged 26, was crushed, left a widow and young family.
- Isaac Watson, aged 27, died at home from broken legs, broken back, and head injuries.
- William Holiday, aged 48, was crushed.
- William Elliot, died at home from injuries after falling down a shaft from the pit top.
- William Shimming, aged 26, died from gangrene six days after being sent home with crushed feet and examined at Jacktrees field station.
- Samuel Leshbrook, aged 32 from Cornwall, died of two crushed legs and broken arm after six days in Whitehaven Infirmary.
- Henry Nicholson, aged 58, crushed to death.
- John Moffat of Penzance Street Moor Row dislocated his elbow when the pit cage tangled with the wall while descending in to the mine. He was sent home to have it put right, on February 2nd 1888.
- John Glaister of East Road Egremont had his broken leg treated at home, after a rock fall had snapped it.

- Isaac Dixon of Moor Row was injured and treated at home in 1881, for severely injured legs.
- The company fined Michael Murphy, engine operator, £5 because they blamed him for the pump beam breaking, when he was earning about £1 a week (value in 2023 about £150 per week).

The disregard to peoples lives started early and displayed industrial proportions in West Cumberland industries. In 1850, before the railways opened up the mines to industrial scale operation, Joseph Nicholson, aged 55, was crushed and killed in Wyndham Pit at Cleator Moor. Thomas Hall, a shaft digger, was killed when the cage rope snapped at Eskett Mine (1852) and he was dropped down the shaft. In 1853 John Kirkby died and three more were seriously injured by a roof fall at Woodend mine. Absolon Devolons, 18, was killed by a roof fall in Cleator Moor mines (1855).

On Christmas Eve 1855 the brutality continued. John Gamwell's wife was widowed, and their four young children orphaned when John was dragged down a shaft and killed when the shaft at Thomas Ainsworth's Cleator mine collapsed.[58]

Two other miners were severely injured but saved themselves by hanging on to ropes. John's body was buried in the bottom of the pit and left there. Fifteen days later, John Gamwells funeral service was held at the pit head by Reverend Leech in front of a large congregation, with his corpse still lost in the pit.[59] The pit shaft was closed but pit props and other equipment were saved for use in other parts of the Cleator Iron Ore Company mine. Twenty four more miners were killed in 15 years in the new mine workings.

By 1856 the new railway was running to Whitehaven through Moor Row from mines and quarries along its route. The same year Joseph Attwood was killed by ore falling down the shaft at Birks mine. Eight more died

---

[58] *Whitehaven Hearld*, 29/ 12/ 1855 'Fatal Accident in an Ore Pit'
[59] *The Cumberland Pacquet*, 8/ 1/ 1856 'News'.

at Birks by 1894, drowned in floods,[60] crushed by wagons and roof falls, or by being dropped down the shaft by winding gear failures. Birks Pit was owned by the Frizington Mining Company, Walker and Piele of Whitehaven were the pits engineers, and James Bateman Kitchin was the Resident engineer.[61]

---

[60] *Whitehaven News* 22/ 11/ 1894: 'Disastrous Flood at Birks Pit'. David Crone, 15; Thomas Toy, 15; David Harrison, 35 all drowned.

[61] James Bateman Kitchin had lived at Moor Row and worked at Ehen Pit, Gilfoot for the Ehen Mining Company, before living at Birks and working for the Frizington Mining Company at Birks pit. He moved on to the Pallaflat mine in 1896, and then the Woodend mine of James Bain and Company as their Agent, in 1902. In 1910 he became one of the five directors of the new Jacktrees Mining Company that worked the Jacktrees mine, formerly the Colorado Pit operated by Carron and Company. 14 people died in the mine, including Mathew Simpson who was found in the bottom of the disused pit 1, thirteen years after he had gone missing after visiting the Three Tuns pub in Cleator. Mathew was never a miner. Pit 1 was next to a foot path and was left open to the fields. [*Whitehaven News* 6/ 5/ 1886, 'Discovery of Human Remains at Cleator Moor'].

Chapter 12

HEALTH AND SAFETY AT WORK

Just outside Moor Row another Ainsworth's pit, later owned by MacKenzies, called Crossfield pit in Cleator Moor also killed 31 in industrial accidents in the mines. Lord Leconfields Crowgarth pit killed seven miners at work, and his Cleator Moor mine killed 20, aged 14 to 57 by 1891. 57 died in Stirlings Montreal mine from 1867 to 1905, aged between 18 to 61. There were over 260 more pits than those listed above, and they all worked to the same standards of safety and management, employing the same sort of people as workers, with the same absence of legal protection and medical support. In the 1830s the Whitehaven News regularly reported workers being crushed to death in mines, yet 100 years later was still reporting them. No lessons were learned, as men went to work like soldiers facing machine guns in some bizarre battlefield, and families were ripped apart and cast aside as the owners resisted attempts to improve safety in case better it would 'encourage idle ways'. There were no official enquiries made in to accidents except an inquest of limited authority that never improved workers chances of surviving to retirement.

Every one of the deaths listed above was judged to be an accident by the coroners inquest. Isaac Dixon of Moor Row was one of those accidents, twice. He was injured by a rock fall in Lord Leconfields mine at Bigrigg on April 4th 1891- in 'an accident that frequently happens' and was treated at home for his injuries. Presumably the Inspector of Mines must have concluded he should have learned his lessons from his earlier experience:

Ten years earlier both his legs were severely injured in a rock fall in the same mine.

In 1974 the UK Government passed a law, the Health and Safety at Work Act, which made it clear that safety at work must be the responsibility of the employer, to stop lives being destroyed by the pursuit of profit. Since then, it is not reasonable to read the accounts of the accidents at work and see health and safety as overkill, a joke or a nuisance. In 1974 over 600 people were killed at work. Since 2008 about 160 people have been killed in work accidents every year in England and Wales.

Chapter 13

THE BEST WAY TO MAKE MONEY IS TO HAVE RICH PARENTS

'Gentry and descent of blood is nothing else but a descent of riches' [62]

Men dream of being able to spend a fortunate windfall, generally on unhealthy living, grand display, and big houses. It is the rich who are remembered in history, because they left behind artefacts and records to be studied. And studying their lives can imply the rich are in some way great, or good, or superior to others if only in the view they hold of themselves. Sadly nothing is known of individual people that lived and worked in Moor Row, except for the barest of data given in government census records or an occasional story in local newspapers. We may know a little of their lives when they acted in concert, as in a war or a protest movement or as miners, but as individual characters they remain as unfamiliar as van drivers passing us on a motorway.

Looking back from 2022 we can see the ambitions and fantasies of people living in the 1850s were, by looking at the life styles of those lucky people who actually enjoyed their fortunate windfall of money and opportunity.

---

[62] John Lowther, (1582-1637), of Lowther Hall, Westmorland. quoted in C.B. Phillips, 'Gentry in Cumb. and Westmld. 1600-65' (Lancaster Univ. Ph.D. thesis, 1973), cited at www.historyofparliamentonline.org/volume/1604-1629/member/lowther-john-i-1582-1637#footnoteref28_1tztp2m

The remains of their fantasies survive in their letters and possessions, and the houses they lived in, of which there are plenty standing around West Cumbria.

The Ainsworths. Six Houses and a Castle

- This family came from Blackburn Lancashire, and owned mills at Preston, Backbarrow, Penny Bridge and Cleator as well as railways, a part share of a shipping line, an engineering company as well as mines and iron factories.
- Together they owned Backbarrow House, Wray Castle and Summerhill near Ulverston in what was then Lancashire.
- In Cumberland they owned Harecroft Hall at Gosforth and Flosh mansion at Cleator.
- In Scotland they owned Ardanaiseig house near Loch Awe.
- In London they owned a house in Pont Street, Chelsea.
- Two of their companies went bankrupt.
- Family members served as Justices of the Peace, Members of Parliament, County High Sheriffs, army officers, company directors, County Deputy Lieutenants, master of hounds for fox hunting packs and President of an Animal Protection Society. They were known for buying Irish foxes to bring over to Cumberland so they could hunt and kill them around Gosforth.
- They employed about 700 people in their mines, iron works and mills, and about one hundred as servants in their houses.
- Their houses would cost about £90 million in 2022. The family sold up and moved to Ireland in the 1920s for the fox hunting.
- The 5th baronet was working for an employment agency in Thailand in 2022.

Ainsworth's Backbarrow House. Backbarrow House was a large early 19th century Tudor styled house of white limestone with gables, mullioned windows and conspicuous chimneys, built to the designs of George Webster of Kendal for the Ainsworth family. It was next door to their cotton mill at Backbarrow. The house was demolished in the 1930s and only the entrance gates remain. The Backbarrow buildings, known as 'Ainsworths' mill locally, were converted in to the Lancashire Ultramarine Factory in 1890, renamed Reckitts 'Dolly Blue' works in 1929 and converted again in to the Whitewater Hotel in 1984.

Ainsworths Summerhill Ulverston. Summerhill is a country house in open countryside close to the Backbarrow mill, and used by Ainsworths when travelling to religious meetings in Kendal. In 2022 it was used as holiday flats.

Ainsworths Flosh at Cleator. Flosh is an old English word for 'bog'. The Flosh was built in 1800 for Henry Birley the owner of the Cleator mill that went bankrupt. Ainsworth bought the mill and the mansion and got supplies of cheap flax from Ireland where he also recruited Irish female workers because they worked for less pay. The new iron businesses led to an increase in people living at Cleator, from 763 in 1841 to 3,029 in 1861. 58% of Cleator residents were then Irish. The house was handed down through the family before it was sold to Cleator Moor council for offices in 1938, then sold again and converted to a hotel.

Ainsworth's Wray Castle Windermere. Wray Castle was built in 1847 for James Dawson, a Liverpool surgeon, and bought by David Ainsworth in 1898. It was sold in 1920 to Noton Barclay by Margaret Ainsworths trustees after she had died. In 1929 Barclay gave the castle to The National Trust who opened it to the public in 2010.

Ainsworth's London House. David Ainsworth and his wife Margaret also had a six storied house in Pont Street, Chelsea, about half way between Buckingham Palace and the Victoria and Albert Museum.

Ainsworth's Harecroft Hall, Gosforth. Harecroft is thought to have been named for Sir John Hare (1603-1637) a politician from Norfolk, whose daughter Elizabeth married baronet Sir John Lowther (1605-1675). The house was replaced when The Hall was built for Samson Senhouse of Maryport (born 1778-1855). John Stirling Ainsworth (1844-1923), later a Baronet, bought and rebuilt Harecroft Hall at Gosforth (Cumberland) and also bought Ardanaiseig in Argyllshire. Sir John owned iron mines and steel making industries in Cumberland. He was Chairman of the Cleator and Workington Junction Railway, and director of the Whitehaven Joint Stock Bank, Member of Parliament for Argyllshire, High Sheriff of Cumberland and Deputy Lieutenant of Argyllshire; Commander of the 3rd Volunteer Battalion Border Regiment; Justice of the Peace for Cumberland and a member of the Royal Commission on Mines. The hall kept 22 servants busy in the house. When Sir John died 24 May 1923, Harecroft Hall, the Flosh, Ardanaiseig House (Scotland) and Thornbank Farm (Gosforth) were given to his son, also called Sir Thomas, the 2nd baronet Ainsworth, (1886-1971). Sir Thomas was so keen on hunting that he bought live foxes from Southern Ireland to be hunted around Gosforth with hounds. Eventually Sir Thomas sold up and moved to Ireland where the fox hunting was better, and he became chairman of the Dublin Society for Prevention of Cruelty to Animals. Harecroft Hall became a school, then was converted in to a camp site with holiday cottages in the barn. The third baronet, Sir John Francis, was a history teacher in Dublin. His brother, the 4th baronet, Sir Thomas David worked in Thailand as a banker. The 5th baronet, Sir Anthony Thomas Hugh Ainsworth (b. 1962), was living in Bangkok in 2022 (Thailand) with his wife Anong Pradith and daughter where he works for an employment agency.

Dalzells of Moor Row, Stockhow Hall Ennerdale, Grange Farm Hayton Aspatria

- The Dalzell family inherited land and a house in Moor Row from John Wildridge, around Church Street in the late 1700s. John and his wife Elizabeth lived with their daughter, also called Elizabeth, on bits of land around the road from Woodend to Keekle and a house on what became Church Street.

- The younger Elizabeth married Thomas Dalzell at St James Church in Whitehaven in 1768, and they inherited the land, house and garden when the Wildrigdes died. Elizabeth and Thomas Dalzell moved to Stockhow Hall at Eskett. In 1798 Thomas Dalzell had a map drawn of his wife's inherited land. Dalzells bought land and property near Sheriffs Gate and at Grange Farm Hayton near Aspatria (126 acres). They owned building land in Moor Row. Their son John was living at Stockhow Hall in 1829. Anthony Dalzell is recorded in 1829 leasing land to Anthony Hill, owner of the South Wales Iron Works called 'Plymouth Works'.[63]

- Thomas Henry Dalzell was described as a civil engineer, iron ore mine owner, and landlord. He was leasing out 'pieces and parcels of land and property of 86 square yards' starting in August 1867. It is Thomas Henry that Egremont Town Council claim a street is named after in Moor Row.[64] John Dalzell (died 1875), of Hayton, also took on leases for building land in Penzance Street and John

---

[63] Cumbria Archive Service Catalogue CASCAT) reference DH/ 132/ 1. www.archiveweb.cumbria.gov.uk. Anthony Hill had also leased iron mines from the Wyndham family, Earl of Egremont and Cockermouth in 1825 (CASCAT DLEC/5/10/1/20).

[64] Penzance Street is reputed to be named after the town in Cornwall, for the Cornish workers who moved to Moor Row. If true it would be unique. Roose near Barrow had 80% residents born in Cornwall in 1881, working the iron mines in nearby Stank. The houses were built by the mine owners to accommodate workers and arranged in two long terraces of 196 houses, called 'North Row' and 'South Row'. Also, in County Durham, there were 4000 Cornish born residents in 1881, living in the 'Greenhill' area. There is a Cornwall Street in Murton, next to Cardiff Street and Corbett Street in the Easington mining region. There was a Penzance Street in Hartlepool, now buried beneath a shopping centre, and a Penzance Street survives in Notting Hill with no known connection to Cornish workers.

Street in Moor Row. His descendants became known as Dalzell Burnyeat. John's trustees owned a 21 year lease to the Moor Row mines from Walker and Peile for £500 annually from 1887, and let them out to John Stirling on an annual lease. The estate included building plots, royalties for minerals in Moor Row, and an interest, with Mary and Richard Studdart Whitesides, in Meadow House in Preston Quarter and the Wheatsheaf Inn in Whitehaven Market Place. Parts of the estate were being sold off by 1885.

- The last known members of the Dalzells of Moor Row are the Rankine-Dalzells.[65] Lady Hilda Gertrude Akerman Rankine died at Hove 1958. She served as trustee to the late John Dalzell's estates in Moor Row and was wife of Sir Richard Rankine, the Governor of Zanzibar, KCMG. Lady Hilda was survived by her grand daughter, the daughter of Sir John Dalzell Rankine KCMG KCVO KStJ and also one time Governor of Zanzibar (officially titled Resident Zanzibar).

Dixons of Rheda Mansion Frizington

- Dixons of The Birks near Cleator Moor acquired Rheda estate by marriage in 1617. The mansion was first built in 1858 and rebuilt in 1881. It was sold in 1950 and later demolished to build a housing estate, although the stable block and Dower house survive at 2022. Thomas Dixon was a yeoman farmer in 1829 who made money by renting land to iron mining companies and being paid royalty money for ore they dug up.

- The Thomas Dixon of 1894 had climbed to Esquire status and become Justice of the Peace and Cumberland High Sheriff in 1887, the year of Queen Victoria's Golden Jubilee. Four years later, to mark the Jubilee, Sheriff Dixons daughter, Myfanwy Holman, nee Dixon, opened the 2 acre Jubilee playing field for children of Frizington to play in, rent free, next to the Lonsdale pit shaft.

---

[65] Descended from Sarah Frances Dalzell.

- Myfanwy married Alwyn Holman, a solicitor whose brother Herbert Leigh Holman married Vivian Hartley who was the famous actress Vivian Leigh that played Scarlett O'Hara in the 1939 block buster film 'Gone With the Wind'. Vivian's residence at Rheda is born out by a surviving medical prescription found on site, made out to her at the mansion's address,[66] and an eye witness account of local residents.[67]

Wilson Fisher and Robert Jukes of Keekle Grove

- Keekle Grove was described as one of the modern mansions in the neighbourhood of Cleator Moor,[68] the other being the mansion at Flosh. The house was built by Wilson Fisher esquire of Whitehaven, ancestor of the Brocklebank baronets of Irton Hall. Wilson had acquired the land through purchase of 112 acres of common land around Whinney Hill from the enclosure commissioners. Whinney Hill was built as a farmhouse, converted to a smithy, then converted in to cottages. Wilson's son Thomas Fisher changed his surname to Brocklebank in 1845 after his maternal grand father Daniel Brocklebank. In 1800 Keekle Grove was owned by Charles Deane esquire, solicitor of London and rented out until after his death in 1865 when his sisters inherited.

- In 1891 Robert Jukes worked as a clerk and lodged with Jackson Sumptons family of 9 people at number 4 Market Street Cleator Moor. By 1901 Robert had moved to Keekle Grove with two servants and was working as a manager at the Cleator iron works. By 1911 he was 54 years old, living at Keekle Grove with a housekeeper, and working as manager of the iron and coal mines in Cleator.

---

[66] In possession of Velda Cook of Moor Row in 2022.
[67] *Whitehaven News* 2nd March 2006; 'The Day I Saw Vivien Leigh in Frizington'.
[68] Caesar Caine (1916) p112.

Galemire Hospital

A hospital was built in 1879 by Cleator Moor, Egremont, Arlecdon and Frizington Local Health Boards with Whitehaven Union Rural Sanitary Authority. It isolated and treated patients with infectious diseases. Originally a wooden building, on land bought from Lindow of Cleator, it was replaced with a stone built hospital, a matron's house, disinfecting house and mortuary. The first Medical Officer was James Syme of Egremont. In 1884 J Eaton, M.D. took over, then his son William Stanforth Eaton M.B., Ch.B. in 1905. The resident staff at Galemire hospital, William and Martha Wilson, were described as 'Master' and 'Matron'.

Gunsons, the Ballantyne-Dykes and the Lindows at Ingwell Hall Moor Row

- Ingwell Hall, which became offices for the Sellafield nuclear business in 1987, was built in 1826 with profits made by Joseph Gunson, a medical equipment salesman who supplied the armies fighting the Napoleonic wars between 1803 and 1815. Joseph Gunson was Company Commander of the British Army Medical Department and he made his wealth by making sure armies were supplied with equipment at the right price.

- There is a story about a military medical manager called Joseph Gunson described in Crowe K., (1976). (Published 1 January 1976), as follows:

There was a Head of the Purveyor's Department in Spain dismissed from HM Services for dodgy work, of the name Joseph Gunson. Previously he had been Purveyor to the forces in Egypt on recommendation of General H Fox, on 20 shillings a day topped up with prize money for property seized by the British when it invaded Malta in 1800. In 1808 he was accused of embezzlement with the Portuguese merchant Lewis Moreira who supplied the hospital. Gunson amassed a huge fortune by submitting false invoices for goods that were never supplied, and pocketed the money put by to feed 45000 patients that never existed. He also kept money meant for the Lisbon hospital expenses for himself. He also changed the regulations to make misappropriation easier by staff officers and was reduced to half-pay in 1814 and then replaced by Purveyor George Dickson who carried on with the abuses. Gunson was dismissed from HM Services for fraud and gross misconduct in 1822. Dickson got the push in the same year as Gunson for the same reasons'.[69]

- The Ballantyne-Dykes family took over the hall before moving to their own mansion, Dovenby Hall, at Cockermouth in 1860. Dovenby Hall became a car garage in 1998 building racing cars.[70]

- Ingwell was occupied by Samuel Lindow, and gifted to his nephew Jonas Lindow Burns-Lindow, born 1838, who also had a house at Irton Hall, Holmrook that he lived in.

The Lindows of Ehen Hall, Old Hall, Croft End, at Cleator, and Ingwell Hall at Moor Row

- Jonas Lindow senior lived in Old Hall at Cleator and had a bacon making business in the village. His family owned the Little & Lindow spade factory at Cleator Forge in 1829. The Lindow family were farmers in Lancashire who went on to own businesses involved in iron mining, steel making, and railways. Jonas seniors grand father, also called Jonas Lindow had married Agnes Matson of Tytup Hall, Dalton in Furness.[71]

- Jonas Lindow senior developed corn mills and owned a forge to make spades at Cleator that were sold to the local mines.

---

[69] www.maltaramc.com/staffmo/g/gunsonj.html
[70] Dovenby Hall had its own private railway station, Dovenby Lodge, for the exclusive use of the Ballantyne Dykes family who served as chairmen of the Maryport and Carlisle Railway. The station is now a private house.
[71] Dugald Lamb, who moved to Dalzell Street Moor Row in 2002, lived at Tytup Hall in the 1990s.

The Lindows owned or leased mines in the Cleator and Bigrigg area and had pits on at least 15 sites. Ehen Hall was one of the houses belonging to the Lindow family at Cleator. It stood in eight acres of garden.

- The Burns-Lindow branch of the family owned iron ore mines at Longlands, Row Foot, Syke House, Pallaflat, Gutterby, Summerhow (Woodend), Jacktrees (Cleator) and Frizington. and owned the Kelton Limestone Quarries. They also took over the Peel pits, and owned residential property in Cleator, Cleator Moor and Moor Row and various farms in West Cumbria including Black Beck Farm and Yeorton Hall Farm, near Egremont.

- Their wealth got them positions of power and influence. The family acted as Justices of the Peace in law courts, they served as High Sheriffs of Cumberland, and as members of Cumberland County Council. Jonas was county councillor for Egremont North, while his father was Medical Officer to Cumberland County Council. Lindows were High Sheriff of Cumberland four times in the 1800s:

    - 1862: Samuel Lindow, of Cleator.
    - 1874: John Lindow, of Ehen Hall.
    - 1877: Jonas Lindow Burns-Lindow of Irton Hall
    - 1883: Jonas Lindow, of Ehen Hall.

The Lindows owned other mansions around Moor Row, like Ingwell Hall and Irton Hall, and the large house Croft End at Woodend over looking the Cleator forge. Thats a lot of houses paid for by making bacon.

Jonas Lindow Burns Lindow, and the Brocklebanks of Irton Hall Holmrook

- Irton Hall was first built as a fortified tower in the 1300s and inhabited by the D'Yrton family who arrived with the Norman conquest of England in 1066. In 1872 the Irtons sold the hall to Mr Jonas Lindow Burns-Lindow, pit owner and business proprietor of Ingwell. He had the house extended.

- Jonas died in 1893 at the house and his widow sold Irton Hall in 1895, to Thomas Brocklebank. Brocklebanks were a Whitehaven shipbuilding family originally from Torpenhow. The first known Brocklebank, Daniel, was born at Torpenhow in 1741. He was an apprentice ship wright in Whitehaven and emigrated to America to build ships at Portland Maine before becoming a gun runner during the American civil war. After losing his own 20 gun brig in action he had boats built by Spedding and Co and Stockdale and Co. He died in 1801 with a fleet of eleven ships and having built twenty seven ships in his ship building yard. He also part owned the Blue Funnel shipping line in Liverpool. The shipping line grew to 50 ships serving China, India and South America.

- When the Whitehaven ship yard closed in 1865 the Brocklebank ships were built by Harland and Wolf in Belfast. The shipping line was bought by Cunard, and finally disappeared in 1983. Successive Brocklebank baronets became Chair of Cunard Line, Directors of the Suez Canal Company, and directors of The Great Western Railway.

- In 2022 the 6th baronet Brocklebank was Aubrey Thomas, born 1952 who studied at Eton and Durham (Psychology) and sits on the boards of eight money lending companies. In 2012 he bought all the London fire engines for two pounds. He races classic Citroen 2CV's for a hobby. Irton Hall was used as a hospital for children with cerebral palsy between 1967 and 1980 and was being used as a hotel in 2022.

Lowthers and The Flatt, Whitehaven

- There has been a building on this site, known as the Flatt, since at least 1692. The property was bought by Sir John Lowther on 1st October 1675, and has been known as 'The Castle' since the beginning of the 18th Century. It remained in Lowther Family hands until 1920. In 1926 it became the Whitehaven Infirmary, until 1964 when the West Cumberland Hospital was built. The Flatt was a geriatric hospital until closure in the mid 1980's. After a long period standing empty the building was converted to private flats.

- Lowthers owned the 400-roomed Lowther Castle at Penrith and the 70 roomed Cottesmore Hall near Oakham in Rutland for fox hunting. The Penrith Castle was left to become a ruin. Cottesmore Hall burnt down to be replaced with a housing estate. The dog kennels were turned in to houses but the Cottesmore Hunt survived.[72] They also owned a house at Carlton House Terrace, next to the Duke of York monument on The Mall between Trafalgar Square and Buckingham palace in London. In 2022 it was owned by an Indian billionaire, whose billionaire brothers own the houses each side as well.

Postlethwaites and The Hollins

- In 2022, the house stands between Manor Gardens and Hollins Close in Whitehaven. The name hollins is an old version of hollies or holly bushes. Miles Postlethwaite of The Hollies (Hollins) near Whitehaven was proprietor of a mine in Moor Row that closed 1929. Miles was born 1858 in Gosforth, after which his mother

---

[72] The hunt was investigated in 2021 and 2022 for cruelty to horses that were kicked and face slapped, and for driving over a hunt protester with a land rover.

Isabella Postlethwaite lodged with Mary Ann Minster at 19 Keppel Street Bloomsbury in 1871[73] with him and his three siblings. Miles died 14th November 1899 in Mombasa, British East Africa after he caught small pox during his grand tour holiday of the world. He left £42,000, and his estate to solicitors. Miles' brother Johnathan was a solicitor and iron ore mine proprietor, of Fair View Lamplugh, also known as Ennerdale Hall

The Stirlings of Park House Bigrigg, Bridekirk House Gosforth, Fairburn Estates Muir of Ord in Scotland, and a five floored house in Chelsea

- Park House at Bigrigg was the first family home of John Stirling and his wife Mary in 1852, the daughter of John Hartley of Moresby House.[74] Their first six children were born at Park Side. In about 1862 they moved to Bridekirk House, at Cockermouth, where four more children were born. Park Side house stood behind what was the Bigrigg petrol station in 2022. The house was demolished between 1900 and 1928, the site becoming Parkhouse mine and then a concrete making works and car garage.

- John Stirling from Craigie worked with his sisters husband at the Cleator Linen Thread Company, later called Messrs Ainsworth and Stirling, then Ainsworth, Stirling and Cuppage, with Henry and John Cuppage as partners.

- In 1853 Stirling set about prospecting for iron ore, to make a fortune for himself. In 1858 iron ore was found at Todholes farm in Cleator only a few feet from the surface. In 1862 he opened the Montreal mine in Cleator Moor, which mined both coal and

---

[73] Keppel Street houses were knocked down. The street is occupied in 2022 by the London School of Hygiene and Tropical Diseases, built 1927 and the art deco Senate House library tower of The University of London, built in 1937.

[74] Later known as the Howgate Hotel. Hartley was one of the owners of Whitehaven Haematite Company of Cleator Moor.

iron ore. Montreal mine had ten working pits between ten to one hundred fathoms deep (20 metres to 200 metres), with an output of 3,000 tons per week. From 1870 to 1880 the mine produced 2.3 million tons of ore. It closed in 1918.

- By 1870 John Stirling, then aged 50, left Cumberland for ever, to live in Scotland. He retained control of his businesses which continued to make big profits for him. His children married families of industrialists and baronets in Scotland. John was a Justice of the Peace at Whitehaven, a keen hunter with the Cumberland Foxhounds and the Whitehaven Harriers and keen follower of curling, as well as being an enthusiastic stalker, shooting man and salmon fisherman.

- John Stirling was never a Cumbrian landowner.[75] In 1876, he bought three Scottish country estates and joined them together to make the one big Fairburn estate near Muir of Ord, with 31 thousand acres altogether. In 1883 the original house was knocked down and replaced with a huge mansion with its own farm, a stable block, kennels and a gate lodge. He planted his own forest of Silver Fir, Spruce and Pine around the house.

- In 1877 he bought a 5 storey house in London, 17 Ennismore Gardens, Kensington (valued at over £50 million in 2020 for the whole house) behind the Victoria and Albert Museum.

- When he died in 1907 he gifted the 2020 equivalent of £55 million pounds of property to two of his sons in Dunblane and Ayrshire while his eldest son William received the Chelsea house and Scottish Fairburn estate of 30000 acres with the castle, worth at least another £50 million in 2020 values.

- The 100 men still working for him at the Cleator factories when he died were sacked.

---

[75] www.cumbrianlives.org.uk/lives/john-stirling.html

Spedding and Summergrove Moor Row

- Five generations of Speddings owned Summergrove mansion since the late 1700s. The Speddings descend from Edward Spedding, a farmer who married Sara Carlisle. They had four sons, one called Carlisle Spedding, manager of the Lowther mines in Whitehaven[76] who was killed by a gas explosion in a Whitehaven mine in 1755. Carlisle Spedding's son James was the first Spedding to live at Summergrove. He bought the estate from Anthony Grayson in 1761.

- James married Lucy Harrington, and the house was handed down through their family to Major James who married Mary Dykes Ballantyne, then to Mr James Dykes Spedding who married Emily Wyndham, then to James Wyndham Harrington Percy Spedding, who died in Capri in 1924 unmarried and with out any children.

- The house passed to his cousin Mark Quayle, and then sold to John Anthony Spedding who lived at Storms near Keswick. After the Second World War the house was sold, turned in to flats and caught fire twice. Spedding made applications to build houses and extend the lodges in the 1960s and 70s, and use the walled garden as a coal depot by Mr Murray.

- In 1982 the building was demolished and replaced with a workers hostel by British Nuclear Fuels.

- Several members of the family saw military service in Europe and the Cumberland militia, notably under the Duke of Wellington in action against Napoleon, or General Abercrombie.

The locations of marriages, christenings, weddings and funerals

---

[76] Edward and Sara's sons were called John, George, Lancelot and Carlisle. Carlisle's brother John worked for the Lowther estates, and his descendants eventually owned the country houses at Armathwaite, Mirehouse (Keswick), Ballynamulagh, and Winderbrowe.

spread across Europe and mention Countesses and Earls amongst their families.[77] [78] The social standing the Spedding family enjoyed is seen in the census returns for the daughters of Major Spedding whose work was recorded as 'Lady' in census records. Their neighbours at Goose Butts and Padstow, were recorded as lime burners, coal miners, carters, labourers, smiths, ore miners, wife, and cobblers.

The Other Speddings of Mirehouse, Keswick

- The original house was built in 1666 by the Earl of Derby as a hunting lodge, and expanded in the 18th and 19th centuries. In 2022 James Spedding said he had lost count of the number of rooms, although Janaki, his wife, is sure there are 67 windows with views of Bassenthwaite Lake.

Paupers and The Whitehaven Work House

- In 1861 the Preston Quarter Work House had five named officers to supervise the 297 worthy poor 'pauper inmates'. George Kelly, a Chelsea Pensioner, was Master, and Mary Kelly his wife was Matron. Isaac Southward was school master, Hariett Mitchell school mistress and Thomas Trohear worked as the porter.

---

[77] Captain John Carlisle D Spedding published his family history in 1909 for Private Circulation '*The Spedding Family*', but now available on the internet! www.ia802704.us.archive.org/23/items/speddingfamilywi00sped/speddingfamilywi00sped.pdf.

[78] There is also an account of the Speddings of Summergrove in 'Cumberland Families and Heraldry', Cumberland & Westmorland Antiquarian & Archaeol.Soc., 1978

Chapter 14

OWNERS COMBINATIONS and WORKERS ASSOCIATIONS

The Kelton Fell Railway

The Rowrah and Kelton Railway that served Knockmurton shows how business owners co-operate and conspire with each other for as much control as possible to protect and improve their profits. The Rowrah and Kelton Fell Railway was three and a half miles long. It never carried passengers but it did affect the lives of all people in the area. Indeed, the experience of West Cumbria gives insight in to the history of British heavy industry growth in miniature form. The study of Knockmurton mines by Hewer [79] exposes in detail the social, technical, economic, and novel problems that need to be overcome to achieve something that seems inevitable now, with the benefit of hindsight. Viewed from a modern standpoint, that privileges interests and ideals of the world we know. This is history is written the winners. As with the history of the medieval period, we know more about religious inquisitors than the heretics they confronted, and more about state officials than their subjects.

The list of special jobs in a work place can be very long. A railway for instance needs something to carry, like iron ore at Knockmurton. The ore needs miners, but first there must be prospectors to find the ore. Then

---
[79] Hewer, R E (1988)

engineers are needed to build the mine, miners to work the tunnels, crafts men to mend the equipment, people giving orders and others counting up what is made and storing the money. Miners need shovels and tools, bought from forges like at Mill Walk Lamplugh. They need houses, and builders to make them. And miners need food and people to grow it for them and even more to sell it to them. The iron ore they dig up needs carrying to the iron works, in trains, wagons or on ponies. And the iron works need limestone, coke made from coal, and more people to work them. Then the finished iron is taken away and made in to tools, weapons, pots and pans. All those people need looking after, by having churches to sing in, hospitals to be sick in, nurses to make them better, and schools to get children ready for working. And some one in charge to make sure everyone else does what they are told and to enjoy spending the money stored up in the bank. Knockmurton had all these elements brought together on a bleak hill side above Rowrah

The first mine owners were called Carmichael, from Rowrah, who rented the land from the Lord Lamplugh. Then John Stirling of Cleator took over, followed by the Scots firm of William Baird. Mine owners often built houses for their workers, as Baird's of Glasgow did at Kirkland. There were 30 company houses built in Kirkland, in five terraces. The influx of people to the area is shown in the 1841 census, and in the 1847 directory of Cumberland, Kirkland is described as a hamlet. In the 1851 census there were 40 separate households with 170 inhabitants. Twenty six of the households depended on farming for their means of subsistence. By 1881 there were 472 people living in the township living in 60 households. Bairds also built railway lines, to Rowrah and Workington. They also owned coal mines, iron works and railways in Scotland.

The hamlet transformed into a cosmopolitan village with people moving there from all over the country including Scotland, Ireland, Wales, Isle of Man, Cornwall, Devon, Cumberland and some one from Russia. And the mine, the railway, and all those 472 residents needed supplying with the all those things that made living up a hill side possible. The village contained:

a dressmaker, tailor, boot and shoe maker, blacksmith, joiner, builder and cart repair business, Alexander Twiname's building contractor and grocery business, a pub (The Wheatsheaf), a Board School and a Methodist Chapel. There was no doctor, no dentist, and no hospital to serve this outpost.

The offices of the Kelton Railway were in Queen Street Whitehaven, and the first directors were James Baird, Robert A Robinson, Alexander Brogden MP, Alexander Whitelaw, Martin Boundy, and William Wallace. William Wallace was the first chairman but died in 1876 and was succeeded by Andrew Kirkwood McCosh (who had replaced Martin Boundy in the first year of the company's existence). James Baird was also the managing partner of the Lonsdale Haematite Iron Company at Bransty Whitehaven. He was also later on (in 1887) a prime mover in the formation of the West Cumberland Ironmasters Association which regulated prices, tariffs and wages to make sure owners co-operated with each other to maximise their profits and rationalised their resource requirements. The other directors had jobs on the side too. Robert A Robinson, of Cockermouth was Chief Agent for Lord Lonsdale and promoter for the Cleator and Workington Junction Railway, Alexander Whitelaw, Great-Grandfather of William Whitelaw MP was once manager at the Gartsherrie Ironworks and a joint owner of William Baird and Company. Martin Boundy was an Iron ore mine owner from Cornwall, and Alexander Brogden, MP for Birmingham, owner of nine houses, and part owner of three railway companies also owned a separate mining company.

The railway closed in 1933 and the line was sold by the Whitehaven Haematite Iron and Steel Co. to Mr J W Kitchin of Moor Row. The track was lifted and sold for scrap in 1934, and the directors and owners of The Rowrah and Kelton Fell Railway moved on to their other businesses. The workers houses were emptied of residents and demolished in the 1930s.

The family of Bairds came from Lanarkshire near Glasgow. The eight brothers were given the business by their father. They were all millionaires in their twenties. They owned two mines in Cumbria, a railway, a railway wagon factory, coal and ore mines in Scotland, coking coal works, iron and steel factories, huge country estates in Scotland with mansions and castles. Bairds also had mining interests in Africa. The fourth eldest son died in 1876 and left an estate worth three million pounds in his will- that's equivalent to £270 millions in 2022. (King Charles 3rd is thought to be worth about £500 millions in 2022). This family of Bairds dominated the area of Rowrah for 40 years, until the ore ran out, and illustrate the total control a business will want to have over an area to establish and sustain itself.

Certainly, any mining company would want to make sure the railway company would not tempt miners with better pay, and the other way around. The best way to achieve this was co-operation about worker pay with companies that might poach workers. Alternatively a company might pay workers a lot more to encourage them to stay on, but this would reduce profits. Kelton Railway was by no means unique, as seen by the joining together of regional railways to reduce operating costs, and by hotel chains, supermarkets, and steel and iron making companies to merge and form partnerships. Indeed co-operation between companies is the rule, although worker co-operation is still treated with great suspicion, as seen by the amount of laws that dictate how unions must behave and how members behaviour must be checked. Yet, the 30 directors of the Cleator and Workington Junction Railway (C&WJR) held ninety other jobs besides the ones at the C&WJR,[80] in companies that were supposed to be competing with each other in markets to give the best price to their customers and best profits to their owners. There is a long history of association between work men being frowned upon, or feared, and laws of

---

[80] McGown Gradon, pp 65-67. The affinity of these other jobs can be seen by the examples of Fletcher of Brigham Hill Cockermouth, MP for Cockermouth and director of two coal mining companies, a second railway, an iron and steel works and was Chairman of Cumberland County Council. Also, McGowan of Rosenheath, director of eight other mining and steel companies, and Sir James Ramsden of Abbotswood Barrow, the general manager of the Furness Railway, Mayor of Barrow, High Sheriff of Lancashire, and director of four other companies.

England used to prohibit work men societies. It was felt worker association was a bad thing because it would undermine free trade, promote anarchy and sedition, and suppress profits. Trade combinations, that is owners co-operating with each other, were thought of as good thing because they 'promoted industrial order and a disciplined regulation of the workers'.[81]

It can be seen that business owners co-operated with each other to make sure they met their demand for profits. Unfortunately in the interests of control they refused such associations with and between the people who did the hard work. Until 1824 worker associations were illegal in Britain, with membership of trade unions being an offence until the 1871 Trades Union Act. From about 1850 unions had organised to improve workers lives with safer working conditions and more secure pay. In 1875 the Conspiracy and Protection of Property Act meant workers on strike could picket the work place without breaking English law. They also campaigned for working people to be able to vote for politicians in elections, which finally happened in 1918 for men and 1928 for women.

Workers Associations and the Cleator Moor Co-Operative

For many years, iron ore miners were not protected by safety laws in the work place, although coal mines were.[82] The laws that did apply to ore mines were not concerned with safety, only with working hours, and the gender and age of miners.

Reporting of accidents at the year end was required, along with productivity records and plans of mines that had been abandoned.

In 1875 there was one fatality nationally for every 390 people employed underground in ore mines. The risk of being killed as a miner was 1 in 10 during a forty year working life in a mine, although most of the deaths were of men under 30.

---

[81] J A McKenna and Rodger (1985).
[82] 85,000 workers died in mine accidents in 80 years from 1873 in the United Kingdom, on average 3 a day for every day in 80 years: www.mininginstitute.org.uk/wp-content/uploads/2016/02/Mining-accidents-and-safety-Jan16.pdf

It has been estimated that one in ten miners died before they could retire, either in accidents or from diseases caused by their jobs.[83] [84] One hundred people died in accidents in Frizington ore mines alone.[85] In 40 years from 1880 at least 23 people died in the Moor Row mines. In 1911 Mr Winston Churchill the Home Secretary was challenged about the safety record of Moor Row mines in Parliament. The example of 8th March 1911 was used to make the point, that when Robert Maxwell had his arm injured at work, it became poisoned. Maxwell was injured when a piece of ore landed on him while he was cutting a tunnel roof. He was off work for a fortnight,[86] incapable of working or earning a living. Yet Churchill thought the mines management was adequate as he pointed out there was no law that required mine managers to be competent or skilled in their job.

Six years later, on January 17th 1917 Robert 'Bob' Maxwell of Bigrigg was killed instantly in Postlethwaites mine at Moor Row, when the mine collapsed after a dynamite blast. David Manders of 46 John Street was witness to the fatality, along with John Payne of 49 Dalzell Street. Samuel James, manager of mine, said 'Bob' was a leading man of the company. Robert Maxwell's father, also called Robert, had emigrated from Londonderry Northern Ireland to escape a famine and provide a safer future for his family. Robert senior is distant relative of Velda Cook and Kristina Cook of Cote Close and Cobra Castle farms on Dent, who moved to Dalzell Street Moor Row in 2002 and to Londonderry respectively. He is also a distant relative of Ian Patton of Harrington who moved to Worcestershire.

Overall there was much more apathy about the dangers than alarm. Since miners were paid for the amount or ore they got to the surface they were

---

[83] Dodd, 2010, p13.
[84] Carlisle Spedding, mine engineer for Lord Lowther, was believed to suffer a breathing disease for years from inhalation of the bad air in mine workings. Eventually, he was killed in a mine explosion caused by gas. Beckett (1982)
[85] Arlecdon History Group; (2017) has a roll of fatalities in the Frizington mines, pp 31 – 42.
[86] https://api.parliament.uk/historic-hansard/commons/1911/jun/19/metalliferous-mines-act-moor-row

not inclined to slow work down to protect themselves, and employers didn't want profits reduced by slow working. The employers excused the indifference to miners safety by suggesting that 'imposing safety measures would merely encourage lazy habits'.

The houses miners lived in were generally rented.[87] Workers could not get loans to buy houses because their work was too unreliable. If work dropped off or a miner was injured they could not pay for their housing. Many owners banned trade union membership under threat of dismissal, which would cost a miner and family their home. Home had two bedrooms, a small parlour, a back room and a kitchen. It was heated with a coal fire. There was no gas or electric. The toilet was an earth closet outside, shared between neighbours. The cold tap, when there was one, was also shared and also outside, as was a coal heated water boiler (called a 'set pot') for washing and laundry. Having a bath meant squashing in to a tin bath in the back room. The streets were surfaced with gravel and cinders with cobbles for gutters.[88]

There were no dentists, no free doctors,[89] and one hospital with four beds for injured miners in Cleator Moor.[90] There are no records of any medical staff working at the mines hospital at Jacktrees. The large population, packed in to over crowded housing, combined with the lack of sewers meant epidemics of infectious diseases were common. Local 'Boards', the early version of local councils, were set up around Moor Row in the 1860s, re-invented as Councils in the 1890s. The Boards were staffed by the mine owners and their managers. They wrote the rules on how town residents must live, concerning themselves with regulation and control of nuisance.

---

[87] Less than 10% of houses were owner occupied, before 1918. See Christopher Powell for instance, in *The British building industry since 1800: An economic history* (Taylor & Francis, 1996)

[88] Arlecdon History Group, (2017), p43

[89] The 1861 *Gazetteer* shows the nearest medical people to be the two surgeons based at Egremont, [Morris Harrison & Co., Nottingham, Michael Moon reprint 2000 p239.

[90] *Whitehaven News*, 5.10.2006.

The rules covered stuff like:
- Building public clocks.
- Stopping causes of nuisances on the streets
- Regulating taxi cabs
- Naming streets and numbering houses,
- Demolishing dangerous buildings
- Fire prevention
- Providing a market place.

The Council published a 55 page book of laws to be followed, which give an idea of living conditions for working people and the issues that concerned town leaders. There were no laws, for instance, about safety at work or about the town, providing health care, and nothing about sanitation arrangements. Some behaviours that were banned as a nuisance were;

- All pigs and swine to be fenced in and kept off the street,
- Rugs to be beaten before eight in the morning,
- No interference with street lamps,
- No wanton door knocking,
- Chimneys not to be set on fire,
- Slaughterhouses to be painted twice a year,
- Rubbish, filth, dust, ashes, snow to be cleared away. [Duffy, p20].

In 1879 the council bought the Carron Iron Company's muddy 2 acre pitch in the centre of town and replaced the pig styes on the land with a new Market Hall. In 1889 the Council refused to close schools to control an epidemic of measles and scarlet fever[91] in the area, which was spreading by school attendance, against advice of the towns Medical Health Officer. There were many complaints about sewage disposal for want of water to

---

[91] Both diseases cause long term health problems if untreated.

flush the street drains. The council's Inspector of Nuisances often found more than overcrowding in houses, like pigs kept inside in larders to be near the fire, and hens kept with the coal under the stairs.

Accounts of hopping in 1890s Cleator Moor invokes feelings of a quaint open air farmers market from 2022[92] in Duffy's description: Butter, cheese, biscuits, sugar, and flour all weighed out loose; No pre-packed goods; No car ride home. There were post offices for savings accounts, postal services, and assurance offices for sickness insurance. There were seven fruit and vegetable shops, nine butchers, five sweet shops, two chemists, three booksellers, four tobacconists, four pawn shops, two cycle shops, four hair dressers, two drapers shops, two iron mongers and two banks. There was also Halls music shop, where a baby grand piano might be bought for fifty five guineas when a miners pay was £50 a year. Not cheap at all, a guinea was 21 shillings, so fifty guineas is the same as £57.75, equivalent to £8,500 in 2022 value.

Cleator Moor was the home of the greatly successful Cleator Moor Co-operative store, started at 35 Ennerdale Road by six residents in 1858. It grew to be one of the largest Co-ops in the north of England and a paragon of collective worker self help in the members lives of grinding labour. The Co-op had branches in Whitehaven, Bowthorn, Ennerdale, Frizington, Rowrah, Wath Brow, Pica, Distington, Bransty, Kells, Bigrigg, Hensingham, St Bees, Cleator Moor and Moor Row.[93] Its shops were the subject of paintings by L S Lowry. It owned a mill and ran a farm. Cleator Moor Co-operative society became a prime example of working people creating a successful association that served their particular interests by application of practical realism. Eventually there were 10,000 members when it combined with the Cumbrian Co-operative in the 1970s, and in the 1990s became an outlet for the Co-operative Wholesale Society.

---

[92] Duffy, (2019); p59.
[93] Duffy, p66. And Marshall & Walton (1991) p135.

Chapter 15

THE NEED FOR RAILWAYS

The country around Whitehaven has many minerals buried beneath it, which have been mined for hundreds of years, usually by just a few individuals at a time. As early as the Roman days in England there was mining and quarrying in Cumbria. Everywhere in Cumbria the waste heaps, broken ground, and remains of old buildings are evidence of people digging for lead, copper, zinc, baryte, haematite (iron ore), tungsten, graphite, fluorite, and coal, and quarrying for limestone, sandstone, and slate.

In 1818, at the ages of 79 and 81, Thomas and Elizabeth Dalzell both died. Their memorial stone at St Bees priory commemorates five generations of Dalzells. Moor Row was still much as it had been throughout their lives. But towns round about, like Egremont, Cleator and Whitehaven were cultivating landowners who were keen to get rich. Up until then, the Cumbrian coast and the North Pennines had been isolated by mountains from main land England except by boat.

The extensive rivers and high rainfalls led to water wheel powered mills setting up to make wool and woven products. Attempts to build factories around Cleator before railways were built often failed, like the Cleator flax mill and iron furnaces at Flosh. Cockermouth had 19 mills at some time or other. The development of steam power meant mills could be built more conveniently near big towns and railways, bringing an end to the Cumbria mills driven by water wheels. With the growing populations and growing size of towns came an increase in need for household goods and industrial equipment, which meant more iron and steel was needed to keep up with the changes in living.

Mechanisation of digging led to the development of bigger quarries and mines. Originally all the stuff dug up was transported to ships using carts and pack horses along tracks or the turn pike roads. This was slow, wasteful and expensive.[94] Building railways made transporting bulky goods like coal to harbours was much easier. The ships took the minerals to factories in South Wales, Newcastle, Chester and Scotland, that converted them to useful metals like iron, copper, lead and so on, using coal to melt the rocky minerals and separate the metals. Lowther recognised in 1805 that a railway to Carlisle would increase profits from his coal mines, when he wrote to the Mayor of Carlisle offering to promote a railway between the two towns.

By 1855 the Whitehaven harbour had reached a limit for ore shipments. The harbour trustees had refused access to Ainsworth's 400 ton capacity propeller driven boats in about 1855 because the harbour could not be made deep enough. But there were still profits to be made from iron, if a way to ship larger amounts could be found. The limit for ships was based on the weight of the cargo and not on the type of cargo, so mine owners switched to converting bulky ore and coal in Cumberland and build iron and steel furnaces next to their mines instead.[95] Once the iron and steel had been made it was sold and sent around the country and the world in

---

[94] The transport between Bootle to Egremont and Whitehaven, was a choice of 8 pack horses a week, returning next day and dependent on the tides around Ravenglass. A steam boat left Whitehaven once each week, for either Annan, Dumfries, Dublin, Kirkudbright and two overnight steam ships ran to Liverpool. Alternatively, it took two days to get to Liverpool by stage coach. [Parson and White (1829), p275.]

[95] In 1867 there were 30 or more ore mines, in what became Cumbria, feeding 33 blast furnaces in the county, i.e. the Furness furnaces at Barrow, Backbarrow, Ulverston, Askam, and the Cumberland furnaces at Millom, Moss Bay, Cleator Moor, Maryport, Distington, Harrington, Workington. One quarter of the furnace output was steel, in great demand even then to make railway track. By 1875 there were over 60 blast furnaces. [Marshall & Walton 1981 p42.]

ships from the harbours or on railway trains, leaving all the waste behind in Cumbria as piles of rubbish. A railway connecting mines and quarries to coke ovens, furnaces and the harbour became vital. And shipping costs would fall because only the smaller volume of finished steel would go on ships or the new railways.

Building railways was meant to improve business because they are suited to hauling bulky freight like coal, from where it was dug up and taken to places it could be sold or turned in to something more useful.

Rail routes can be laid to run close to major customers, through local depots and goods yards, and on to international shipping ports. They allow many users to access the network by simply adding more wagons and more rail, and can be added to bit by bit as needed by adding a junction and some lengths of track.

Railways are also good at carrying large amounts of bulky goods over long distances. The idea to carry passengers was at first a way of making extra cash for very little extra cost.[96]

Railway building had come late to Cumbria compared with the rest of Britain, and that meant industrialisation was twenty to thirty years behind the rest of England.

The Senhouse family of Maryport promoted the idea of building a railway along the Cumbria coast, and encouraged building the railway between Carlisle and Newcastle that opened in 1838. That railway was built to carry coal from Newcastle to the Irish Sea for onward shipment to Ireland and Wales or Scotland by boat. Cumbria landowners also saw the opportunity to get their minerals to ports cheaply and reliably, so they could join in the get rich schemes spreading through the north of Britain.

---

[96] The very similar Furness Railway carried 12,000 passengers between Dalton and Piel pier in its first two months of working in 1846, even though the primary purpose for the line was '...to improve the present very dilatory provision for the transport of the valuable Mineral products of Furness and adjoining Districts to the Coast" as advertised in the *Lancaster Gazette*. 9 December 1843. "Furness Railway", p1.

In 1847 the railway connection between Carlisle and Whitehaven was opened, and in 1850 Whitehaven was linked to Barrow in Furness. The Whitehaven tunnel was built in 1852, and Barrow was connected to Lancaster in 1857 giving connections to railway main lines, south to England, north to central Scotland, and east to Newcastle and county Durham. Whitehaven and the west coast was then connected to the rest of Britain. Moor Row was connected to the national rail network in 1855, when it became possible to buy a train ticket in Moor Row for the ten hour journey to London.

Chapter 16

MOOR ROW JUNCTION

The railway from to Moor Row from Corkickle to Egremont and Frizington was built to serve iron ore mines at Bigrigg, Cleator Moor, Woodend, and Frizington, plus the ironworks in Cleator Moor, and lime stone quarries at Eskett near Rowrah. The newly formed Whitehaven Cleator and Egremont Railway (WC&ER) Company built, owned and ran the railway. It was predicted the line would carry 100,000 tons of ore a year to Corkickle. The line opened in 1855, and by July 1858 was carrying 6,500 tons of ore a week to Whitehaven for shipment to Wales.

The railway yard opened to goods trains in 1855 and became the centre of a network of industrial lines that served coal, ore and stone production. The station opened to passengers in 1857. Collapsing mine tunnels caused subsidence damage to a viaduct near Egremont, but within 15 years the company was making so much money there were extensions built to Sellafield from Egremont and to Marron Junction from Rowrah. The yard and station at Low Keekle was called Moor Row Junction on the 1863 Ordnance Survey map, surrounded by terraced houses at Scalegill, Station Terrace, Railway Terrace and cottages along the Woodend to Keekle road. The houses were mainly occupied by railway workers and their families. Moor Row was, therefore, in its beginning a railway town built to provide homes for railway workers. By March 1882 the *Whitehaven News* estimated the WC&ER Company was serving 280 pits along its routes, and two more railways had opened, between Cleator Moor and Workington and between Rowrah and Workington. There were other mines that delivered ore to rail heads using horse drawn carts and over head cable ways[97] like at Bigrigg.

The railway served the following iron mines in Moor Row,

- The Bigrigg Mining Company's Sir John Walsh[98] mine with two pit shafts that worked from 1882 to 1939,[99] first opened by S and J Lindow.
- Anthony Hill's[100] Robin Benn mine with two pit shafts, later run by the Workington Iron and Steel Company working in the 1800s.
- Two single pit shafts called 'Billy Frear' and 'Barker'.
- Miles Postlethwaite's[101] mine with two pit shafts, working from 1892 to 1929.
- Thomas H Dalzell's Moor Row Iron Ore Mining Company of three pit shafts, worked 1881 to 1925
- The John Stirling mine of one pit shaft, working 1881 to 1925.

---

[97] Cited in Mervyn Dodd ; *The Story of Iron Ore Mining in West Cumbria*, 2009, p10.
[98] Sir John Benn Walsh is the 1st baronet (1759 - 1825), born as John Benn, son of William Benn of Moor Row and Robin Benns brother. He adopted his wife's uncles name of Walsh to inherit his 'considerable' fortune and lived in Berkshire. The inheritance in 1800 is the equivalent value of £33 millions in 2022. The 2nd baronet Sir John Walsh (1798 – 1881), became Baron, the Lord Ormathwaite. There is a Robin Benn mine shaft next to the Sir John pits behind Hollins Park. Barons' Ormathwaite served as High Sheriff of Berkshire, High Sheriff and Lord Lieutenant of Radnorshire and sat as Members of Parliament. They are related by descent to the 14th Earl Home, called Alex Douglas Home who was Prime Minister in 1963.
[99] When the ore ran out John Walsh shaft pumped water away from the Bigrigg mines to stop them flooding. Pumping was stopped in 1939, when the mine water then drained to Longlands flooding the field to form a lake.
[100] Anthony Hill (1784 – 1862) inherited the Plymouth Iron Works at Merthyr Tydfil that produced over 35,000 tons of iron a year. Hill signed a lease for ore mining at Moor Row with Anthony Dalzell in 1829.
[101] Miles Postlethwaite (1857 to 1899) was John's son, and lived at Hollins mansion in Whitehaven. He died on holiday in Mombasa, Kenya while touring the world. The mine was operated by his executors after 1900. Postlethwaite also worked the Fletcher Pit near Bigrigg from 1888, which closed in 1915 and abandoned in 1929.

The Stirling pit shaft is under Montreal Place; the Moor Row Iron Ore Mine pits are in the swampy ground behind Pearson Close and each side of the Woodend Road near Blind Lane and 'High Lodge' house. Miles Postlethwaite's three pits stood in the field between the Woodend road and the gravel track that leads to Hollins Park, next to the Barker and Frear pit shafts. The railway built a Bigrigg branch to serve 48 more pits around Bigrigg, Woodend, Clints, and Longlands, which ran across the Woodend road at Quaker Bridge.

West Cumberland iron ore became expensive because it was hard to find underground and needed deep mines to get to useful amounts. It was hard to break in to small enough bits to pull it through the mine tunnels and haul it up the pit shaft. Shipping the ore from West Cumberland to where it could be made in to iron or steel, was also expensive. There were other places to get iron ore from at much lower prices once the special properties of Cumberland ore for steel making was no longer needed.[102] The amount of ore dug up in West Cumberland reached a peak in the 1880's and thereafter declined to almost nothing by 1920 as iron from other sources could be used much more cheaply to make steel.

The Gilchrist-Thomas steel conversion process was invented 20 years after Bessemer developed steel making using low phosphor iron ore from Cumberland. After a late start in industrialisation, caused by poor transport links to the rest of Britain, the Bessemer process had caused a rush for Cumberland to be the major supplier of a pure iron for making steel. But within twenty years, the new Gilchrist-Thomas converters meant the Cumberland landowners game was up, and they would have to find new ways of occupying their time in their London villas and Scottish mock castles, apart from counting money piling up. There would be a few years left to clean out the mines of easy winnings, but not enough money left to clean up the mess.

---

[102] Cumberland ore was the main supplier for making steel using the process invented by Henry Bessemer, because of the very low level of phosphorous impurities. Sweden was also a world leader in making steel. Once a Phosphorous tolerant process was developed steel makers could buy ore from just about anywhere.

Working conditions in mines were extremely hard and dangerous. In 1880 miners in Frizington were striking to reduce their underground shifts of 14 hours a day, to ten hours a day[103]. The work of these 'red men', covered in grime from the red ore, involved hand drilling with a springer[104] and hammer, splitting rock with wedges, blasting with dynamite, hacking at loose rock with picks, and shovelling shattered rock in to trucks on railed tram ways. Air in the tunnels was so stale that candles sputtered or went out. Meals of sandwiches were eaten on the job with cold tea reheated in a tin over the candle. Toilets in the mines were a wooden barrel painted with tar, or a private corner in the rock.

Miners were not given safety equipment, and made do wearing old clothes that got soaked in wet tunnels, especially when floods broke through the wall or roof of a working. They wore clogs of wood because sharp rocks would split and cut leather, and packed them with straw as socks because it dried quicker than wool.

From 1841 the population of Cleator and Cleator Moor grew from about 900 to over 9000 in 50 years as the advantage of Cumberland iron ore was taken to the limits by the local mine owners. As the iron mines ran out of easy pickings, the owners ran out too. In the next forty years to 1931 the population of Cleator Moor dropped to about 6000 people. The same decline in work and population happened throughout the mining and steel making areas of West Cumberland, as jobs disappeared and unemployment rose to 40%. The government of Britain stepped in to prop up steel making for war making in the first world war, which had 5000 working in the mines. There had been a brief surge in profits around 1924 when 3000 miners were working, and owners complained they should not have to pay Excess Profits Taxes.

In the second world war the government propped up the mine owners again, while 1600 miners worked underground. Simply put, with out the demands

---

[103] Barber p12.
[104] A long hand held drill bit, struck with a big hammer, needing two people to make a hole or split the ore under ground.

of a war for steel at any price, Cumberland iron ore was too expensive to sell. In 1904 it was six times the price of ore from Northamptonshire, and in 1930 it was still over three times more expensive than competitors prices.[105] Unfortunately the effort did not prop up the towns above, which began collapsing in to the mines as ore pillars were removed holding the tunnels up beneath Cleator Moor town centre. Monreal Street and the school were the most renowned losses. Mine closures followed for 40 years. Some shafts were kept open to pump flood water out of mines still lifting ore, until finally in the 1980s they were all closed down and left to drown.

In 1849 100,000 tons of Cumberland iron ore were hauled to the surface in to the light of day,[106] for the first time since it was formed 500 million years earlier. By 1870 one million tons was being pulled up, more or less every year until 1920, followed by the long decline to half a million tons in 1942, down to 250,000 tons in 1963, then roughly 130,000 tons each year from 1970 to 1975.

---

[105] In 1904 Cumberland ore sold for 8 shillings per ton (£58 in 2022 values), compared with 1 shilling 6 pence per ton (£10 in 2022) for Northamptonshire ore. In 1930 Cumberland ore sold for 17 shillings per (...contd...) ton compared with between 5 to 6 shillings per ton from other suppliers. [Barber, p23].

[106] Sugden, E H, (1897) p105. Lists the main owners of 1847 as Ainsworth at Cleator, Anthony Hill at Bigrigg, Lindows at Gutterby, Tulk and Ley at Yeathouse, and Attwood at Woodend (sic). Tulk and Ley were also owners of the Lowca engineering works from 1837, and had bought the Seaton Iron Works that Richard Spedding had built, son of Carlisle Spedding. Lowca works were started by Heslop and Millward in 1794, then Tulk and Ley, then Henry Fletcher, Jennings and Company from 1857. Henry Fletcher lived at Croft Hill at Quality Corner off Red Lonning Whitehaven with his wife, five children and four servants. Fletcher and Jennings featured in the fictional stories of Rev W Audrey as the builders of the locomotive 'Rheneas' in The Railway Series and Thomas and Friends. Fletcher and Jennings built over 200 real locomotives, and was renamed Lowca Engineering when Henry retired. In 1858 Lowca built locomotive 21 for the Whitehaven, Cleator and Egremont Railway that ran through Moor Row, later called 'Keekle 100A'. They built 'Wyndham No. 178' for the Kelton Railway in 1880. The engineering works closed in 1927. In 2022 Croft Hill was a guest house with 5 guest bed rooms for about £100 each per night. Three Fletcher locomotives still running are 'Baxter' on the Bluebell Railway, and 'Talyllyn' and 'Dolgoch' on the Talyllyn Railway.

The highest annual amount was in 1881, at 1,615,635 tons[107] of ore, that is just ten years before the 1891 census list of Moor Row residents given earlier. The workers and their families who made it happen were eventually put out of work and on to welfare payments or zero hours jobs with zero prospects. Just as the mines were designated as 'abandoned' when they closed, there must have been many families who felt the same.

Many miners went overseas to work in South African diamond and gold mines, or America. The grand houses were sold, closed up, converted or demolished as owners abandoned the area for better prospects outside Cumbria. They left behind spoil heaps, flooded broken ground, waste lands where buildings stood, and fetid pools pretending to be nature reserves.

The remaining artefacts around Moor Row are railway bridges carrying the cycle path leading out of Cumbria to Sunderland, the cracked seven arched Keekle viaduct that took the railway between Cleator Moor and Workington, a stone crusher at the site of Montreal Mine pit 4, a railway signal post and overgrown platforms, the 'black ships' of Keekle Beck that kept the river out of the mines at Moor Row, and river aqueducts at Longlands, Yeathouse and Parkside. And the stone built terraces built for workers cottages with the chapels where they could pray for salvation, handy for work and now the nucleus of a new Cumbrian 'exurb' since the 1990s.

---

[107] Data from Appendix 3 of J Y Lancaster and D R Wattleworth, (1977).

Chapter 17

MOOR ROW HOT SPOTS

Quaker Bridge for an Anabaptist Minister

On the road to Woodend, at the dip that floods after heavy rain, there was a railway bridge crossed the road to the mines around Bigrigg. The railway was built over a former non conformist cemetery in the corner of the Sepulchre Meadow shown on Ordnance Survey map published 1867. The remains were exhumed and moved to another cemetery and a memorial stone left in the earth embankment to John Garner.

Locally the bridge was called 'the Quaker Bridge', but Quakers do not ordain pastors or build monuments to their dead[108]. Caine's research shows John Garner was an Anabaptist minister, not a Quaker.

The War Memorial

On Church Street is a granite celtic cross that records the names of fifty four Moor Row and Scalegill people killed in the 1914- 18 and 1939- 45 wars. It was unveiled in 1921 by the Moor Row school headmaster Mr H Bonney, on land gifted by Mrs Thomas Postlethwaite of Hollins mansion in Whitehaven. It was dedicated again in 1948 by Regimental QMS J K Thompson, RAMC.

---

[108] Caesar Caine 'Cleator and Cleator Moor Past and Present', 1916 and 1973 reprint p308.

Longlands Lake

Longlands Lake is formed from a flooded mine. Water leaks in to mines from the ground above. In the 1920s when Longlands iron mine closed and the water pumps were turned off, water filled the mine and then flooded the ground above as the mine tunnels collapsed under the field. There are remains of some mine buildings at the Egremont end of the lake.

At Longlands the mine was protected by straightening the River Ehen and putting it in a concrete channel next to the road to Egremont. The mine had pumps to keep the water level low enough for men to work in the tunnels. Four people were killed in accidents in the mine between 1894 and 1924, when it was abandoned.

Black Ships and Boilers and a Metal River

In Moor Row, The Black Ships are the 500 metres long concrete troughs built to hold water in the River Keekle and stop it breaking in to the Montreal Mine underneath. The mine's number 12 shaft was in the field next to the Black Ships, almost at river level and used to pump flood water out of the tunnels.

At Frizington, a large iron pipe was made to carry the Windergill stream waters above the Margaret and Agnes mines near Yeathouse station, called the Boilers. At Parkside Bridge the Lingla Beck was stopped from flooding the High House mine east of the road at by a 'metal river', a new river bed made of metal trunking, still there in 2022.

Rock Crusher

The rock crusher, a great lump of iron machinery, stands above the cycle path to Keekle from Moor Row, made of iron with two drive wheels and gears to grind stone in to pebbles, stands close to where Number 4 Pit of Montreal Mine is buried.

Just around the corner on the path to Cleator Moor is a sandstone chair with an inscribed poem about the mines and miners around Moor Row.

Chapels

The Methodist chapel and Sunday school on School Street corner with Penzance Street have been replaced with a bungalow. The houses on the opposite side of Penzance Street are the last terraces built in Moor Row.

The former chapel on Church Street is a motor garage. The chapel and Sunday school on Scalegill Road have been converted in to houses, facing the turn in to Hollins Park.

There used to be a railway workers mission opposite Scalegill Place which became a lock up garage. The mission was to provide spiritual support to railway employees, and encouragement to abstain from drinking alcohol by the local temperance society.

Village Hall

The village hall stood in Penzance Street, and hosted the party in 1953 to mark Queen Elizabeth 2nds coronation. It was converted in to three houses overlooking the school play ground, retaining the Flemish window in the gable end overlooking Penzance Street.

Dalzell Street Chicane

Originally Dalzell Street crossed the railway at a gated crossing next to the station, so that the road was straight. The bridge was built later, next to the crossing, which is why the road is kinked over the bridge.

The roads from Scalegill Place, Keekle Terrace and from Scalegill exactly follow the ancient earth tracks from before 1800, before even wheeled carts used the lanes which were the preserve of pedestrians and an occasional donkey. In 2015 Cumbria Highways Department recorded 14000 motor vehicles travelling over the Dalzell Street bridge each week, 10000 of which were speeding at over 30mph, and 1000 were heavy goods vehicles [Reeves, for Cumbria County Council, 30/07/2015].

The sandstone bridge parapets stood for 150 years before they got knocked over by a van turning in to Railway Terrace side and by a tractor on the opposite side of the road.

Station Terrace

The line of conifer trees facing Railway Terrace grow on the site of Station Terrace houses, which were knocked down in the 1960s. Trains for Whitehaven left from the platform next to the conifers. The platform had waiting rooms, a ticket office, station masters house and signal box. A foot bridge crossed the line for Cleator Moor bound passengers on the other platform, whose remains are still there. The last foot bridge was brought from the Lindal in Furness station when it closed, and then reused at Kirkby in Furness when Moor Row station closed.

Railway Yard

The concrete yard over the road bridge was for goods sheds, engine sheds and workshops for the railways, and rolling stock sidings. After the railway closed a fencing contractor used the yard as a store.

In 2022 the eastern end of the yard and the neighbouring field are recorded as High Risk Areas for development purposes by the UK Coal Authority[109] due to under mining tunnels. There are plans to build houses on the site.

There are areas of Cleator Moor that have the same dangers due to mine workings at Bowthorn, Crossfield, Norbeck and Parkside on the road to Frizington.

Railway to Pearson Close

The hump in the field between Dalzell Street and the school is the remains of a railway line that connected the ore mines behind Pearson Close with the Whitehaven to Cleator Moor line. The railway crossed the field on an embankment, ran across Dalzell Street to where the entrance to Pearson Close is in 2022, and then turned toward Woodend for a few hundred metres.

Egremont Town Council rented the ground between Penzance Street

---

[109] The interactive map can be viewed at https://mapapps2.bgs.ac.uk/coalauthority/home.html. See also https://www.gov.uk/guidance/planning-applications-coal-mining-risk-assessments#check-if-your-site-is-in-a-high-risk-area-on-the-coalfield

and the railway for allotments. The council then rented the allotments to people in Moor Row.

There were allotments behind John Street too.

Moor Row's Members of Parliament

In the 1922 general election Thomas Gavan Duffy won a seat in Parliament for Whitehaven, and again in the 1923 election to serve under the Prime Minister Ramsey McDonald, the first Labour party Prime Minister of the UK. His offices were at Alva House Moor Row.

He was Secretary of the Cumberland Iron Ore Miners and Kindred Trades Association for 23 years. To learn how mine owners ran their business he bought shares in the Workington Iron and Steel Company which owned mines in Moor Row. The union office eventually moved to Bowthorn in Cleator Moor.

William John Dalzell Burnyeat of Moresby Hall was grand son of Thomas and Elizabeth Dalzell of Moor Row and Stockhow Hall. He served as Liberal MP for Whitehaven between 1906 and 1910.

The End of Hunting With Dogs

Newspaper reports of the hunts in the 1780s say two thousand people on foot and horse back would take part in a days hunting between Monkwray and Bigrigg. Hunting with packs of Harrier and Beagle dogs declined after the 1850s, by which time Mr and Mrs Ainsworth would lead fifty hunts men on foot led by 12 or so red coated men and women[110] on horses.

By 1901 there were no hedges left in the area for hares and foxes to live, so the pack of dogs that formed the Whitehaven Harriers hunt were sold off. The land was crossed with railways, walls and fences around mines and factories which also put the dogs off the scent of any fox. The noise and filth of mines and furnaces must also have combined to distract the dogs and deter the fox. In 2022, children and the rambler have replaced the fox as the bane of the land owner. Perhaps they will be hunted down instead.

---

[110] Caine, 1916, p394.

Mine owner and master of hounds Thomas Ainsworth had kept his hounds at Cleator behind Kennel Cottages, on Kiln Brow (called Ivy Cottages in 2022). James Palmer, village black smith of Kiln Brow and keen hunter, a neighbour of the mansion at Flosh, lived at Dog-Kennel court near the Hare and Hounds beer house. The court became Palmers Court in tribute to his personality in his lifetime though he never owned it or built it. The Hare and Hounds still stands, as a private house, with a lintel over the door inscribed 1731. Water for villagers was carried in buckets up steps from the river, through Palmers Court, before a piped supply was installed.

The water at Moor Row was drawn from a well at the junction of what is now Dalzell Street and Church Street, when only the building in the area was the Wildridge home stead.

Train Explodes in Moor Row

In 1872 a locomotive driver was killed when the steam boiler of his engine split and exploded, throwing a 2 metre by 1 metre strip of heavy metal 30 metres in to a field. The driver died instantly when struck on the head with pieces of flying metal. The train was standing at a stop signal just through the Dalzell Street platform, on its way to Whitehaven, at about 7:00 o'clock in the morning.

Two crew members escaped any injury because they had just climbed down from the locomotive and walked back 15 metres toward the station when the explosion happened. The locomotive, a Stephenson 6 wheel saddle tank engine, had done 250,000 miles in ten years and passed all its inspections.

Steam Roller Crashes Through Bridge

In the 1940s Dalzell Street was having new tarmac laid, which used a heavy steam roller to compress it to make a smooth surface. As the roller passed over the railway bridge the driver was taken ill, and the out of control vehicle drove through the bridge wall and crashed on to the railway below. It lay on the track for a few days waiting for a crane to lift it back on to the road. Luckily no one was hurt.

The crash site was a major attraction. While the roller was recovered school children came from Egremont, including the future Egremont Rugby Union star Ralph Edmunds. Ralph's family were long time residents of Moor Row, and he moved to 22 Dalzell Street with his wife Betty when they married in 1958 after he had done his national army service.

Houses

By 2022 almost all the houses of Scalegill standing in 1891 had been knocked down and replaced with modern houses. The 6 houses of Gutterby, 4 houses of Fishers Court, 11 houses of Station Terrace, and the Moor Row station buildings had all been demolished. Two farms had been lost from the village to new houses at Larch Court and Hollins Park.. The original farm buildings of Thomas and Elizabeth Dalzell from 1800, recorded on his estate map, are also lost under the houses on Church Street facing the former chapel on Penzance Street.

After the First World War the English government was concerned about diverting working class people away from protesting about living conditions. One urgent concern was the price and bad condition of housing, which needed government help to sort. Homes for Heroes was a popular newspaper headline in 1918 which made clear how important a home is for everyone. [111] The old terraces were in general small and lacked facilities. They were built with substantial walls and double pitch roofs that have survived the test of standing over 100 years, even though they were built under pressure to get houses built quickly to let businesses grow. Overall the original cottages give the village centre a uniform sense of drabness, like many other villages of the period in the region. There are no details to compete with the pillars, porticoes, mouldings and gardens of either the mansions and middle class houses or the fore courted municipal town halls, schools and libraries. They look remarkably like miners houses throughout England from the early to mid 1800s- small roomed terraced cottages, low ceilings,

---

[111] There is lots of material on the promises of home provision. One easy introduction is Trevor Yorke *Homes Fit For Heroes*, (2017), Countryside Books. Sadly decent homes have been the subject for many government speeches but very little government action.

small windows, four rooms, shared facilities, built of local stone, with the barest plot of land outside, all thrown up on bleak exposed moors.[112]

Despite the overall similarity of houses, Dalzell Street houses have detail differences. Some have passages that led to the back garden, others had extra upstairs windows, some front doors are on the left of the house, others to the right. Some have bedrooms in the attic. There are some that have a stone hood and label stops above the door way. One has a bay window, and another faces a different way to the other 65 houses. One house has an integral coach porch, although there is no record of what it was for. One house has a date stone. The terraces have a lot in common. They are built from the same sand stone, with the same stone mullions, sills and jambs, and originally had the same stone roofing cover. They were left with bare stone walls when built. Inside they were built using the same pattern doors, door latches, architrave and skirting boards, brad nails, same floor and roof beams and the same size floor boards. Originally they were all finished with lime based plaster to the inside walls and ceilings. They are all roughly the same size, arranged on two or two and a half storeys. But although they are of a common form, they were not built in one go. There is about 30 years from the first and last terrace house being built. Short sections were added as more people moved to the village. Irregularities between the terraced cottages show the points where building work either paused or was done by different builders.

Dalzell Street, Penzance Street and John Street have become outwardly more similar in 2022 as many of Dalzell Street have been rendered with wet or dry dashing. Houses in other streets were covered in render to protect the stone at the time they were built, except for a few on John Street. There is a wider variety of detailing to house frontages than on Dalzell Street: Some on Penzance Street share features of houses on Church Street and Scalegill Road- they stand back behind front forecourts, with dormer windows to

---

[112] For example, Chapel Street in St Just Cornwall, complete with Methodist chapels; or the Rhonda valley in Wales, MacNeill Street in Larkhall, and Waldegrave Terrace in Radstock Somerset.

set them apart, having stone string courses, hood mouldings to windows, as well as bay windows, and a service road at the back to take rubbish away. These may have been built by speculative builders looking for higher prices as employment became more secure. Modern picture windows have been fitted to some houses, sometimes where a house was being used as a shop. The drains taking rain water over the pavements were made locally at the Heathcotes foundry in Birks Road Cleator Moor- the name is still visible, cast in to the gulleys.

Modern houses show similarities and differences too. The bungalows of Pearson Close, built in the 1980s, are similar to those on West Spur from the 1960s, except how far set back from the pavement they are, and the distinguishing roof of mock Roman cement pantiles or thick grey cement slates. Brick panels at Pearson Close provide relief to uniform dry dashed walls at West Spur. Hollins Park houses from the 1990s are also set apart by the finish to the outside walls in the understated style of 1980s beige terraces, sliced up like a Swiss roll cake, and fitted out with low cost roasted honey mock oak cabinets and doors. The jumbled Larch Court, built around 2006 for managers and masquerading as fake country cottages for executives, is characterised by irregular building lines and open plan gardens, topped off with a confusion of gabled roofs. The cul de sac is unified by the common brick tone and roofing tile. The road, paved with block paving and protected by traffic calming humps, provide an unwelcoming impression of private space in the public areas, making up for a lack of playing room in the small gardens and giving an open outlook across the street to give an illusion of spacious front courts.

Rusper Drive, being built in 2022, will be set apart by the giant glass windows that take up entire walls to the roof line and the jarring confusion of angles the houses face the street with. They are the progeny of could-be-anywhere brick boxes packed with miniature bedrooms surrounding a statement entrance hall. Open plan living has made a comeback. But the designs are ambiguous and lack character. They are neither modern, traditional, nor ecologically sound.

None of these new developments make the idea of quaint old little England village life of sales brochures a reality; no warm conversations at the front step, no community spaces for swapping gossip, no entertainments or events, shops or services like a doctor. There is an absence of any ecologically inspired transport system for old, young, or infirm people, that gives any protection from bad weather connecting to anything worth going to. In the era of global climate change concerns, there are no heat pumps, renewable energy sources, low carbon materials, and even no electric car charging points. It is as if the village has missed out again on main land England's obsession with environmental challenges facing everyone else in the world.

Lost Footpaths

Dalzell Street south side is shown on official maps to have a path running along the back yards- the gates for the yards are still visible in the walls, but the path has disappeared. There was also a path, shown on maps, running from Dalzell Street to Scalegill Place past Alva House and Victoria Villas, that had also disappeared by 2002.

One path shown on official maps runs from John Street to the former Sir John Walsh mine, around the edge of Hollins Park past four capped mine shafts. Another path runs from the war memorial to St Johns church, across fields. It starts at Church Street, passes through Hollins Park, and turns over the field from Larch Court. Such paths criss crossed the area around West Cumbria and were called 'Church roads'. The Church Street path also runs from Dalzell Street, and down behind Pearson Close, used by miners to get to work in the iron mines around the River Keekle. The swamp is a legacy of bad twentieth century building practices and unlawful tipping of rubbish. It once provided good pickings for scavengers looking for old glass medicine bottles, cordial and pharmacist poison bottles until the potential for accidents became a serious worry.

There is another Church road that runs from Gutterby to St Leonard's church in Cleator. Buried beneath the Leconfield Industrial Estate is the route of a Church road from Bowthorn farm across the Moor at Cleator that was closed off to stop locals using the route to church. The iron works had built over the path in the 1840s, and eventually the owners were concerned about site security. Likewise a number of paths have been lost by destruction of stiles and being over ploughed or over grown by hedges.

Unfortunately the Cleator Moor iron works owners security concerns did not extend to the safety of nearby residents. On June 9th 1857, six people from three households died overnight as they slept.[113] Fumes had leaked in to their houses from blast furnace slag tipped against homes. At the inquest in to the deaths, the iron works and the house landlords contested the post mortem findings, until a government scientist pointed out that the houses on Bowthorn Road were dangerous to live in precisely because of poison gasses leaking from iron works waste in to the houses.

Sinking Buildings

The mines have a reputation for swallowing buildings. Places like Jacktrees farm and Fawn Cross farm,[114] Cleator Moor central train station, Montreal school and the surrounding streets, the main road at Bigrigg approaching Clints Brow, Longlands lake, and back gardens in Howbank Road Egremont are some sites that achieved notoriety for disappearing in to old mine workings. High House farm was demolished as it started to sink, at Parkside, and rebuilt some distance away, to be safe from ore mining.

The irregular brick work to the Parkside railway bridge crossing the road to Frizington bear witness to the attempts to repair the damage caused as the ground kept sinking beneath it.

In Egremont, nine houses were demolished in 2007 after mine workings collapsed around them in Greenmoor Road. In 2012 houses on Howbank Road were evacuated for some weeks after gardens sank in to mine workings. The original cap at Ulcoats mine near Egremont is visibly sinking, and the Fletcher pit shaft cap near Bigrigg collapsed in 2018 leaving the shaft open to fly tippers. The nearby Sir Johns pit of Moor Row was reckoned

---
[113] Members of the Sloane, Fenton and Armstrong families of Birks Road died.
[114] Duffy 2019 p131.

then to be 40 metres deep to the water filling the tunnels.

Moor Row Awards

- In the 1950s Moor Row was nicknamed 'Jam City' because village children recycled the most glass jam jars in the region. [*Whitehaven News* 20/ 10/ 2011]

- In 1953 Moor Row won the worlds biggest bottle of beer for the village coronation carnival. The bottle held 1800 pints of Newcastle Brown Ale.

- In 1979 Moor Row won a national newspaper competition for being the top British venue for the Queens Silver Jubilee parties, the prize being pop, cake, and a brass band from The Sunday People newspaper.

- In 1997 local residents campaigned for measures to reduce the speed and amount of traffic using Moor Row as a main road. In 2016 local residents campaigned again for measures to reduce the speed and amount of traffic using Moor Row as a main road.

- In 2011 Moor Row was hailed as one of the top ten family friendly places to live [*Whitehaven News* 29/ 9/ 2011]

- In 2014 Moor Row was in the top ten attractive places to live in Britain. [*Whitehaven News* 28 October 2014].

Mine Caps

There are stone cairn caps to mine shafts at Moor Row, and Cleator Moor. A shaft top with its original cap and vent in place is in the fields at Ulcoats mine near Haile. There is a notable depression around the cap, where the ground is sinking in to the pit shaft. Also, 'The Big Hill' wood land park at Ennerdale Road near Wath is the remains of the Todholes iron ore quarry of Cleator.

Railway Paraphernalia

The Cleator Moor bound platform is all that remains of the Moor Row station, with a pile of clay bricks where the signal box once stood. There is also a railway signal post near Alva house and the Needless Beck culvert beneath the Needless Bridge. Toward Whitehaven is the Scalegill Hall cattle creep beneath the railway track bed on the descent to Mirehouse.

Scalegill Bridge Bench Mark

The main A595 road bridge over the old Whitehaven Junction railway has an Ordnance Survey flush bracket bench mark below the painted road engineers reference number. The bench mark is number 10925, and marks the height as 66 metres above mean sea level at that point.

Scalegill Hall

The hall, on the main road past Moor Row, has a Grade 2 listed garden wall and is a Grade 2 listed building itself, although in poor condition. It is a large house, extended and modified over its life, and thought to date originally from 1615 given by a date stone on out buildings . It was originally a home stead built with rubble walls, corner quoins, mullioned windows, lugged and corniced architrave to main door, with a graduated slate roof, the walls covered with protective render.

Chapter 18

CUMBRIA INDUSTRIES

Cumberland has seen the decline of heavy industries as modern methods became cheaper than old production methods used in Cumberland. The effects of World War I and the global depression of 1929 had a major impact on employment in West Cumbria with places like Maryport and Aspatria suffering 30% or more unemployment. From 1934 there were many attempts to bring new enterprises to West Cumbria. By the year 2000, the manufacturing capacity of the whole of Britain was vastly diminished, replaced by "service businesses". This change was reflected in Cumbria where in 2019, manufacturing (4.9%) and Construction (11.9%)] accounted for only 17% of the 23,585 medium and large businesses, with manufacturing generating £3 billions, that is 27% of the Gross added Value of the County. The other 70% of value in Cumbria came from service based work. Some of those industries are listed below, with some surviving to 2022.

Numerous industries were closed from 1900 around West Cumberland, and some survived. Here are a few of the more well known ones:

- Mining of Coal, Iron and Lead. Maryport Coal mining, the last colliery closed in 1967. Whitehaven Coal Mining, the last colliery, Haig Pit, closed 1985. Iron Ore Mining finished in 2007 in Egremont.

- Coke manufacture.

Cumbria Industries

- Weaving, milling, spinning, hat making, leather tanning.
- Iron & Steel producing pig iron and steel rails. Modern railways wanted longer lengths than could not be rolled at Workington. Barrow Steel making finished 1984.
- Calder Hall nuclear electric power station, closed in 2003.
- 13 Electric power stations were built between 1890 and 1925 at Whitehaven, Cleator Moor, Sedbergh, Workington Siddick Colliery, Millom, Penrith, Keswick, Kendal, Flookburgh, Barrow in Furness, Carlisle and Grange over Sands.
- Windscale plutonium factory for nuclear weapon, closed 2022.
- Copper mines at Coniston.
- Lead mines throughout the region, the nearest being at Kinniside on Dent.
- Crane manufacture by Cowan Sheldons closed at Carlisle in 1987.
- Heavy engineering at Vickers Barrow making artillery, railway locomotives, cruise liners, tankers, cement kilns, ; now building only nuclear powered submarines.
- Ship building at Whitehaven and Harrington. Ship building at Maryport between 1765 and 1914 declined due to the ships having to be towed to Glasgow, or the Tyne to have the boilers and engines installed.
- Millom 1971 to 1982 at Sealand hovercraft factory.
- Oxley Electronic Components at Ulverston since 1942-making military electronic components.
- Shepley Engineers of Manchester.

- Clark Doors industrial door design, at Carlisle.
- Millom Hosiery 1948 became Elbeo, closed in 1993.
- Textiles by Ferguson; at Holme Head mill, Carlisle.
- Harris family Derwent Mill for flax, at Cockermouth, closed 1934.
- Carlisle Dixons, Shaddon Mill, taken over by Todds in 1883, who later moved to Loughborough and production went overseas. Mill converted to flats and part of Cumbria university.
- Camtex Fabrics Lillyhall.
- Whitehaven Uniform makers, Turner & Whitehouse who made military dress uniforms from 1940.
- Anhydrite and Gypsum quarrying at Cocklakes Long Meg, Kirkby Thore
- Quarrying of granite & limestone at Shap.
- Slate at Burlington quarries in Furness, and at Honister in Borrowdale.
- Biscuits by Carrs, now part of McVities.
- Cheese making, First Milk Creamery: wholly British farmer-owned dairy co-operative.
- Rowntree chocolate factory at Egremont.
- Penrith Poultry production since 1950's as Frank Bird (Langwathby).
- Food manufacturing, Cavaghan & Gray bought by Northern Foods (1998) bought by 2 Sisters Group; the largest employer in Carlisle in 2004.
- Carlisle Nestle's.

- Quaker Oats mill at Whitehaven harbour.
- Breweries at Barrow, Ulverston, Workington, Cockermouth and Whitehaven.
- Pencils by Derwent Pencils of Keswick.
- Carpets by Goodacres in Kendal, now Cumbria Wool Shed.
- Millers shoes at Cockermouth.
- Brannans thermometers at Cleator Moor
- Kangol hats and safety belts at Cleator.
- Sekers silk and rayon mill at Whitehaven.
- West Cumberland Filters at Cleator Moor.
- Marchon soaps factory Whitehaven.
- Leather work: Shoes by K Shoes of Kendal, joined Clarks shoes in 1981. Last shoes in Kendal were made in 2003. Also in Askam and the Egremont shoe company. Haverigg, Egremont and Whitehaven leather tanneries, with over 100 in Cumbria in the 1800s.
- Sports shoes 1982- New Balance Trainers from Flimby, worn by Rihanna.
- British Cellophane Works, Barrow, opened 1957, and closed 1994.
- Paper making by Croppers. Beetham Paper at Waterhouse Mill.
- Wooden Bobbins.
- Copperas manufacture for sulphuric acid.
- Salt works at Barow, Whitehaven (closed 1770), and Crosscanonby

- Gunpowder manufacture around Haverthwaite.
- Snuff, around Kendal.
- Artillery test firing at Bootle and Blitterlees.
- Tile and brick makers at Frizington, Barrow, Whitehaven.
- Workington Board made cereal packets started in 1966-now owned by Iggesund Paper Board.
- Smurfit packaging at Whitehaven.
- Flexible packaging Smiths Bros Whitehaven
- Cockermouth Gaskets 1969- James Walker Motor Sports Engineering
- M-Sport Dovenby car builders.
- Pirelli tyres 1968 at Carlisle
- Logistics 1940- Eddie Stobart; HGV distribution around country; as Stobart Group into rail freight and aviation (Carlisle, Southend airports and flights.
- Leyland bus factory at Distington.
- McMenon Engineering instruments and pipe work at Workington.
- Turbines by Gilbert, Gilkes and Gordon of Kendal.
- Distington Engineering
- Aspatria Mattresses 1974, later Silent Night.
- Nuclear material transport from 1975 by Pacific Nuclear Transport owned by Sellafield.

- Metal manufacture Cowan Sheldons Heavy engineering closed 1987.
- Design and manufacture of Flow and Temperature measurement products 1948- Fischer & Porter
- Agriculture; the 1901 census showed 17,276 workers in Cumberland and 6,634 in Westmorland. About 13,000 are employed full and part time in 2020 in Cumbria, formed from the two counties.

New Industries

- Wigton Sustainable cellulose films became Innovia Films owned by Canadian CCL making a polypropylene film used for banknotes.
- Off-shore engineering 1965- Lawson Engineering
- Nuclear Decommissioning Agency Nuclear waste clean up.
- Kendal Power distribution & protection Anord Mardix
- Ulverston Pharmaceuticals, started 1948- Glaxo
- Walney Offshore Wind farms, largest in world in 2011
- Forth Engineering at Cleator Moor provides 'bespoke solutions to problem statements'!
- Barrow Pulp & paper mill at Kimberly-Clark tissue paper.

Major Service Industries in 2019

The major service businesses are:

- Health Services: Main Hospitals and District Hospitals and GP Partnerships, ambulance services, hospices, and CHOC.
- Education: in Primary, Secondary, Technical & vocational schools; and at first degree level.

- Councils, including: General public administration activities, National Government Operations, and Regulatory functions
- Social work: activities with or without accommodation for the elderly and disabled, and all social care work.
- Police & a prison at Haverigg: Public order and safety activities
- Transport: Land, sea & warehousing by Stobbarts and Burridges.
- Retail: sales stores with food, beverages or tobacco predominating and Wholesale operations.

Chapter 19

THE HISTORY OF MOOR ROW'S FUTURE

Moor Row is closely comparable with many nineteenth century industrial rural towns found throughout Cumbria, middle Scotland, Cornwall and Durham. They share the characteristics of being substantially built villages of small cottages that have been over taken by the recession of industries that brought them in to being. The collapse of iron mining near its peak in Moor Row has left streets looking curiously lop sided: John Street and Scalegill Road never did get terraces built on each side of the road. The destruction of business premises has led to a village with no centre, leaving it self consciously set out but with no obvious purpose. It lacks the superior air of the theological school town of nearby St Bees. There are none of the frills and embroidery seen in Georgian Regency display at Whitehaven, no market place bustle of Egremont the market town, and none of the discipline of a red brick railway town like Barrow in Furness.

The village is marked by the over bearing utility of its origins, laid out on the old tracks between Woodend, Keekle and St Bees formed by sheep, cows and people plodding along between fields long before houses were built. It can feel like a ship wreck of terraced housing washed up on a swampy island of sieves and rushes, where sea gulls are more at home than sheep.[115]

---

[115] Land around Moor Row was classified in groups 4 and 5, 'Poor' and 'Very Poor', in the Agricultural Land Classifications of the Ministry of Agriculture Fisheries and Food, 1975.

Old mines double as swamps of cankered water and unofficial rubbish tips.[116] The shops that served the village have closed. Walking down rows of sandstone terraces in Moor Row in 2022 it is easy to get a whiff of the rural atmosphere. The Working Men's Institute has survived as a municipal amenity and a play ground stands next to the school, but the street lighting is commonly provided by private residents: Occasional community street lamps merely serve to make the darkness more dismal. The local council refuses to provide this basic public amenity that Cleator Moor and Woodend have enjoyed for over 100 years. Despite the anonymous steel and glass concoctions at the Science Park, the village itself, built on the crest of a wave of the science and technology of iron production looks nothing like the remains of a Victorian silicone valley. In 1911 50% of the workers of the Cumbrian coast worked in iron and steel manufacture, ship building and the associated mining and quarrying industries. Since then the area has limped along with fragile job prospects and subject to perpetual decline. Even at its height of industrial output the area was unacknowledged as nationally important and, as work declined, the area was abandoned to the remedy of workers leaving the area to escape unemployment. The small proportion of the national work force affected by the lack of jobs around West Cumbria do not yield enough votes in elections to change a government means under employment in the area barely gets noticed. In 1921, 20% of the male work force left Cleator Moor for work outside the county. The trend continued as unemployment rose above 20% in 1922 and above 30% in 1931.[117] There was little or no help from national government and little or no protest from residents and social leaders.

Such docility was unusual in earlier years. The settlement of migrant workers provoked protests and hostility in Barrow, Cleator Moor and Millom during the late 1800s. Anti Irish sentiments fuelled accusations of local men losing their jobs. In Barrow in Furness during 1864 dockers drove Irish men from the town using sticks and rocks in response to their reputation

---

[116] Like the collapsed shaft cap that has exposed Fletcher pit to tipping.
[117] Jewkes and Winterbottom (1933) page 69 to 77.

as cheap labour. Similar conflicts occurred in the docks of Glasgow and Greenock, in Whitehaven, and throughout England including farms in Kent. In Cleator Moor during a march of the Combined Orange Lodges of Cumberland in 1884, shots were fired as Irish Catholics defended themselves from attack by Orange Order members armed with swords, spears and guns.[118] On that occasion nineteen year old Henry Tumelty, a Cleator Moor post office worker, died from a gun shot wound.

West Cumbria has clearly severely suffered the effects of the general industrial decline of Britain, made worse by its reliance on the dominating power of a single industry. In its early days, the reliance on one industry could be seen when successive generations followed their parents and grand parents down the mine, in to the steel works or ship yard or on to the railways. This reliance on single large employers exposes any area to capricious behaviour.

Historically the steel industry ran West Cumbria for the interests of the steel industry owners. The same is seen in coal mining and ship building areas.[119] In 2022 a single industry still dominates work prospects around Moor Row but also during the planning of local medical provision, roads and community amenities. This reliance makes far sighted planning an impossibility when trying to rescue an area from an economically inescapable condition. A large employer will dominate planning decisions to protect its own needs, not to serve local residents. The same dominance was established by national government over Barrow, when the shipyard was ordered to build only Royal Navy nuclear submarines or be shut down, effectively bribing the towns people to vote for the government that pays to build war ships in the ship yards, or face destitution. Candidates in elections in the 1800s bought voters with pork pies and beer, and now 200 years later votes for government are bought by handing out government defence contracts. This dominance corrupts voters choices, because they

---

[118] A modern account is given in the *Whitehaven News* of 3rd August 2008 '1884: the day religious divides spilled over in to violent riots'.

[119] Single dominant employers can be held in check. For instance, the Shetland experience of oil wealth management makes a powerful case study of how wind falls can be sustainably invested. 'Shetland Shows the Way to Oil Wealth' in *The Scotsman*, letters, 16/ 08/ 2011.

are pressured to choose between providing for their family or voting with their conscious. One reason for the successful industrialisation of Cumberland was the political control local landowners wielded, through representing their interests in Parliament as MP's on the best terms possible for the owners. Workers who were brought in to the area suffered terrible conditions making a hand to mouth living that was predicated on not falling ill, not being injured and not protesting their living conditions. The boom period of 1850 to 1880 was managed as a personal get rich quick scheme, was not sustained, and has never been reproduced. By 1910 adult under employment and prolonged wide spread youth unemployment was becoming normal. It was only demand for steel at any price in two world wars that offered any sort of redemption.

Not everyone suffered: The Lowthers made the modern equivalent of £9 million from West Cumbria between 1869 and 1878.[120] The Wyndhams of Petworth, headed by Lord Leconfield, made the same amount each year from their Cleator Moor estate, to be spent on the palace of Petworth House in Sussex. The amount of cash removed from Cumberland was considered extraordinary even at the time.[121] It appears that as Lord Lowther and Lord Leconfield grew old they simply lost interest in Whitehaven and Cleator Moor. Once the basic town centres had been set out and the train tracks laid there was little left to engage their imagination. As the ore ran low the attractiveness for doing business ran out, and the business owners ran off with their winnings. By contrast the mineral owners of Furness, the Duke of Buccleuch and Duke of Devonshire, spent useful amounts of their profits locally on supporting ship building works, dockyards, mills, bigger steel factories, air ship factories and extending the railways and quarries. They also developed trading links to America, and laid out a town six times larger than Whitehaven, at Barrow in Furness. The new town in the

---

[120] Lowther accounts are held at Carlisle Records Office. Between 1869 and 1878 the income averaged £60,000 per year, and the equivalent value for 2022 is derived from the cumulative inflation rate of 14,000% [www.in2013dollars.com/uk/inflation/1880].

[121] The 1885 Iron and Coal Trades Review commented that 'no other county returned such vast sums to the mineral owners as Cumberland had' [Lancaster and Wattleworth, 1977, p13].

south of the county worked with a centrally developed plan for the whole area with schools, hospitals, libraries, social housing, brick works, tram ways, tree lined streets, public baths, sewers and sewage treatment works, water distribution, gas supplies, electricity power stations, street lights, rubbish collection, crematoria and cemeteries, piped water to households, promenades and public parks.

Since about 1910 West Cumbria has become a tax payer funded job creation site propped up by international conflict and militaristic language [Barber, 1976]. Just as the recession in steel making started to bite a second time, West Cumbria's remoteness brought industrialists escaping air raids in the south of England, to take up factories on government sponsored industrial estates making armaments,[122] soap, fertiliser, fire lighters, parachutes, and upholstery. In the 1950s the remoteness was used to justify building a factory to make material for nuclear bombs. By 2022 the Sellafield nuclear site was closed to new work and was being washed out and decontaminated to be made safer. The work will last 100 years, employing 11000 people while supporting over half the jobs of West Cumbria. The owners expect a 3000 reduction in work force by 2027, in an area where employment growth is already slower than the rest of the UK. The Sellafield work is estimated to cost between £150 billions to £250 billions at 2022 values. There are no prospects for the area getting jobs in businesses expected to show growth in the future. Jobs in professional services, and information and communication management are either under-represented or non existent in the area.[123] The future for West Cumbria seems to be mainly room service work in either tourism, or hospitals, and local council offices or in a coal mine producing coking coal for the extinct UK steel industry.

Ultimately, West Cumbrian wealth relied on the need for steel made from its haematite ore, which disappeared when cheaper ores were found to

---

[122] For example, artillery firing ranges at Bootle and Blitterlees, Sekers silk factory, Marchon Products, Cumberland Curled Hair, Vickers Armstrong warships and artillery works, Edgards air crew clothing, (...contd) High Duty Alloys air craft parts, as well as a surge in demand for coal, iron, and tungsten from West Cumbrian mines.

[123] Oxford Economics 2017, p3 and p23.

be suitable. The long decline that followed was retarded only by British wars,[124] in Europe and throughout its empire. The local drive to make the money in West Cumbria came from local families who, through old connections, formed themselves in to money making companies with like minded men. Not all these businesses survived for long, and very few survive today. Soap powder factories, mills, shops, making buses and railway locomotives, chocolate, shoes, pencils, railway tracks, clothes, are all businesses that may come and stay, but have mainly come and gone.

Modern businesses behave like ships tied up in a harbour loading up with cash, for just a while only. Once the fundamental reason for being there has gone the ship sails away. Since iron ore ran out the fundamental reason for doing business in West Cumbria has been dominated by decisions taken by a finance committee from somewhere 'down south' to please the accountants of a government subsidy scheme. As long as this remains the case West Cumbria will continue to be weak in jobs and poor in opportunities. It has no real control of its own destiny, being reliant on a London based government that decides where government will spend tax payer subsidies after identifying which areas it needs votes to stay in power. It is unlikely manufacturing industry will ever recover to employ as many people as it did before the 1970s, or offer the job security that such industries bestow.

The impediments to improvement in the area are not easily reversed. The remoteness of Cumbria and lack of any local market for products and services means transport is paramount for employment prospects to improve. The West Cumberland Development Company made this point repeatedly, in 1938, 1948, and 1951, that road and rail links were inadequate,[125] and that fundamental factors like electricity and water supplies, education, housing and social amenities were inadequate for any ambition to improve the area. Electronic communications can be added to the list of failings in 2022. The conscious efforts in the past to break

---

[124] In the 100 year from 1801 there were just 20 years when the British Army was not at war, having fought in 35 conflicts for 80 years of the century. In the 1900s Britain kept out of wars for 36 years in 100, being involved in 22 armed conflicts.
[125] G H J Daysh: (1938) p169.

the 'one industry, one class' character, of the region by building industrial estates has been frustrated by poor transport links.[126] Road improvements proposed in 1951[127] have taken over 70 years to be adopted, and then only with bypasses at the bottlenecks of Egremont, Distington and around Carlisle. Even in 2023, the Whitehaven relief road is no nearer to being built, nor any proposals to improve the Bootle, Holmrook and Calder Bridge bottlenecks described in 1951. Instead the national government acknowledges that poor transport in Cumbria acts as a serious constraint on £25billions of planned investment in the county's energy businesses[128] without giving any hint at how it might be improved.

The government established a Transport for the North Agency that will develop 'multi modal transport corridors between the east and west coasts of England, to facilitate transformational economic growth', without explaining what that portmanteau phrase might mean, and without identifying how nuclear waste plant clean up will improve advanced manufacturing and health innovation industries in Tyneside on the east coast. A similar business corridor is planned for rail connections between Carlisle, Manchester and Sheffield, yet the plan specifically rules out High Speed trains stopping in Cumbria. Increases to rail services, improvements to new roads, or provision of an airport in Cumbria all fail to be mentioned. There is a total absence of plans for the tourism development that has been promoted since the Napoleonic wars of 1800 kept the aristocracy at home in England instead of touring the continent on their 'Grand Tours'. The small number of people affected by fragile employment prospects simply do not attract the political support that cities like Manchester, Birmingham, Newcastle, etc., when the national government is firmly lodged in London.

This neglect of economic prospects for Cumbria extends to the near total absence of cultural pursuits, like live stage productions, museums, music venues, major sports events, and exhibitions. In itself, this betrays the low attention given to the people of Cumbria by London based government.

---

[126] G H J Daysh, (1945) para. 13.
[127] G H J Daysh and Watson (1951), p124.
[128] Transport for the North (2019), pp112, 127, 129 & 137.

The nearest central university campus is 50 miles from Whitehaven, at either Durham or Lancaster, acting as a tourniquet for educational aspiration. The region has almost regressed to the early 1800s or earlier, when compared with the rest of England, relying on heavily subsidised owner operated home stead businesses of the sort raided by Scots Reivers in the 1500s. A narrow hospitality sector fights to compete with much warmer climates and more sophisticated tastes while a policy of UK food self reliance will not improve agricultural prospects based on unimproved land.

The case for better links to outside the county has been made periodically for one hundred and seventy years, from canals and toll roads, to shipping piers or harbours, railways, motorways and airports, yet transport arrangements are still criticised for their inadequacy to encourage new businesses to the region, and for the stagnation in social conditions and family life. In 2020 there were plans to upgrade road links south of Whitehaven to facilitate development at the Sellafield nuclear site. A new road was needed for construction purposes, but no new road was forthcoming. Subsequent planning applications for new roads required the station plans to be approved first. Even as Prime Minister Johnson promised eight new nuclear reactor in eight years,[129] the regions plans for prosperity are held hostage in a political game of blame shifting about when best to make decisions within the five yearly election cycle.

Just as the Reivers raided the county to carry off sheep, cows and gold plate, so too have a succession of industrialists moved in, pillaged the county of its riches, and cleared out, right up to the twenty first century from the fourteenth. In short, West Cumbria faces the same disadvantages from its location and uncertainties in its government as it ever has done, as it struggles with the decline in fortunes from industries in recession since 1911, and cleaning up the wastes. There are no signs of any improvements in regional management, that suggest 110 years of planned and closely managed decline will never be reversed. What a waste.

---

[129] www.gov.uk/government/news/nuclear-energy-what-you-need-to-know published 6 April 2022, from The Rt Hon Kwasi Kwarteng MP, and the Rt Hon Boris Johnson MP.

Plate 1: Station Terrace, Behind Moor Row Station, Looking Toward Cleator Moor.

Plate 2: Mineral Railway Crossing Dalzell Street to Moor Row Iron Ore Mine Pits 3 and 4.

Moor Row in 1891

Plate 3: Moor Row Iron Ore Mine Pit 4 Building and Chimney Visible Beyond John Street

Plate 4: Traction Engine Crashes from Dalzell Street Road Bridge.

Appendix 1

Naming Of Mines

Mines are often named for landowners, or the nearest town such as Frizington and Moor Row, or the name of the mining company itself, and in some cases the landowners wife.[130] Some mines were named euphemistically, like 'Cat Gallows' and 'High Bottom Level', or for some feature in the land, like 'Hole Gill' and even inspirationally like 'Adventure'. Finally there might be a superficial rational naming method using letters or numbers of pits, mines and shafts, although they are not necessarily applied in any rational order like date of opening or depth of workings.

Confusion also comes from mining companies use of the words 'mine' and 'pit'. Most mines consisted of numerous shafts, and at some a shaft or `Pit` might be given a different name from that of the surface mine. There was a Wyndham mine at Egremont and one at Bigrigg, completely separate mines some miles apart.

If a mine was sold the new owners would in some cases change the name of the mine whilst keeping the shaft names as before.

Some of the horizontal ore bodies were so large that they were worked from a number of mines and numerous shafts. For example Crossgill, Parkside, Frizington Parks, Goose Green and High House mines worked the same body of ore which extended over 16 hectares. In later years Beckermet, Florence and Haile Moor mines were worked as one mine.

---

[130] Margaret pit named for Margaret Ainsworth, wife of the owner.

Appendix 2

Mines Within 5 Miles of Moor Row

Arlecdon	Cleator Moor	Egremont	Lamplugh
Birks	Berriere	Bigrigg Mine	Eskett Mine
Cross Mill	Bowthorn	Croft Pit	Eskett Quarry
Dalemellington	Cleator Moor Iron Mine	David Lawn Mine	Kelton Quarry
Frizington	Crossfield	Fletcher	Stockhow Quarry
Goose Green	Crowgarth	Lang Horn	Margaret
High House	Gutterby	Moss Bay	Murton and Coronation
Lonsdale	Hope	Pallaflat	Salterhall
Mowbray	Postlethwaites Moor Row	Florence	Winder
Parkside	Whinneyhill	Ullcoats	Windergill
Threapthwaite Colliery	Park House	Beckermet	Lonsdale Minerals
Agnes	Sir John	Haile Moor	Kelton Fell Mine
Cleator Mine	Woodend	Winscales	Knockmurton
Cleator Glebe	Wyndham	Clintz	Townhead
Lindow	Dalzells Moor Row	Ann	Wreah Pit
Parliament Pit	Gill Foot	Longlands	Todholes Quarry
	Helder	Mildred	

Appendix 3

Notes On The Ownership Of Mines.

The management of mining is split between royalty owners that own the stuff underground, landowners who own the ground that we stand on, mining company owners who sort out the business of making cash from mining, and mining contractors who do the work of digging. These could all be the same, or all different and the names do not necessarily show how ownership is spread about.

The case of Martin Boundy at Kelton serves to illustrate how owners like to separate a business in to little bits. Boundy ran a mining company near Croasdale on a near square plot of land with 1kilometre sides. The plot was managed in two parts, on the east side by 'The Lonsdale Red Haematite Iron Ore Company, and by 'Ennerdale Number 1' Mine on the west. The land itself was owned by Lowther Lord Lonsdale.

The Lonsdale Red Haematite Iron Ore Company also used the names 'Lonsdale Mines KF', or ' Lonsdale Haematite Iron Ore Company', and 'Red Haematite Iron Ore Company KF'.

Ennerdale Number 1 mine was split in to two, called 'Adventure K F' to the south, and 'Boundys Mine' to the north.

All the mines above were owned by Boundy originally, and presumably had different names to keep their money separate in case one mine turned out to be useless and any losses of money would be limited. The mines were worked alone by Boundy at the start and then by eight men who dug about ten feet of tunnels each week. The east side was soon leased to a Mr Dobson, with Boundy staying on as manager. Boundy kept control of the two west side mines, and built wooden huts for up to 20 workers to live in. The two west side pits were reckoned to be raising 10 tons of ore each day in 1874, 8 years after mining had started.

The ore was stockpiled because of muddy roads, and the mines closed for four months because they flooded in rain storms in 1875. Boundy was involved in the Knockmurton and Kelton Fell Railway being built in 1877 and served as one of the directors.

Boundy sold up due to ill health to the Bairds company. He had expected to be raising 50,000 tons a year from the mines, but by 1879 just 700 tons a year was being dug up, and nothing by 1882, seventeen years after he fist had moved in. He did not starve. He stayed at home in Liverpool and watched over his copper mines in Ireland, that were still working in 1892 near Belderrig County Mayo.

Appendix 4

Mine Owning Companies in 1901

There were about 4000 men working underground in 1901 in the 42 mines listed below [Bulmer, 1901, p85], and 1000 working above ground. They raised approximately one million tons of ore in the year, worth about £100 million at 2022 value.

OWNER	NAME OF MINE	LOCATION
LORD LECONFIELD, WHITEHAVEN	Bigrigg Mine	Bigrigg
	Church	Cleator Moor
	Crowgarth	*do*
BLENGDALE MINING COMPANY, GOSFORTH	Blengdale	Gosforth
CROSSFIELD MINES, CLEATOR MOOR	Crossfield	Cleator Moor
CLEATOR MOOR IRON ORE COMPANY	Cleator 6 pit	Cleator
	Cleator 24 pit	*do*
	Cleator 21 pit	
PARKSIDE MINING COMPANY WHITEHAVEN	Crossgill	Frizington
	Parkside	*do*
	Winder	Winder
ESKETT IRON ORE COMPANY, WORKINGTON	Eskett Park	Eskett
POSTLETHWAITE ESKETT MINING COMPANY FRIZINGTON.	*Eskett Park*	*Eskett*
	Postlethwaites Eskett	*do*
WYNDHAM MINING COMPANY, EGREMONT	Falcon	Egremont
	Salter Hall	Salter
	Wyndham	Egremont

Moor Row in 1891

OWNER	NAME OF MINE	LOCATION
CHAS. CAMMELL COMPANY, BIGRIGG	Frizington Park	Frizington
	Mowbray	do
	Park House	Bigrigg
GILLFOOT PARK MINING COMPANY, EGREMONT	Gillfoot Park	Egremont
S AND J LINDOW, CLEATOR	Glebe	Cleator
	Longlands	do
	Rowfoot	do
	Sir John Walsh	Bigrigg
	Syke House	Bigrigg
FLETCHERS HIGH HOUSE MINING COMPANY, CLEATOR MOOR	High House	Frizington
DALMELLINGTON IRON COMPANY	Holebeck	Frizington
CANON COMPANY	Jacktrees	Cleator Moor
WILLIAM BAIRD AND COMPANY, ROWRAH	Kelton	Lamplugh
	Knockmurton	do
LONSDALE MINING COMPANY, WHITEHAVEN	Lonsdale	Frizington
CLEATOR IRON ORE COMPANY	Margaret	Winder
JOHN STIRLING	Montreal 4, 6, 9 pits	Cleator Moor
	Montreal 5, 10, 12 pits	do
EXECUTORS OF T H DALZELL	Moor Row	Moor Row
MOSS BAY IRON AND STEEL COMPANY, WORKINGTON	Moss Bay	Woodend
NEW PARKSIDE MINING COMPANY	New parkside	Frizington
MILES POSTLETHWAITE, WHITEHAVEN	Postlethwaites Moor Row	Moor Row

Mine Owning Companies In 1901

OWNER	NAME OF MINE	LOCATION
WILLIAM LAYLAND, KESWICK	Riggs Head	Borrowdale
SOUTHAM HAEMATITE COMPANY, WHITEHAVEN	Southam	Bigrigg
ULLCOATS MINING COMPANY, WHITEHAVEN	Ullcoats	Egremont
SIR JAS. BAIN AND COMPANY, HARRINGTON	Woodend	Woodend

The above list is not exhaustive. For instance Fletcher and Miller's Agnes Pit at Arlecdon is not listed, although it had changed owners to Postlethwaites Eskett Company by 1894 when William Ray was killed there [Whitehaven News, 5/ 7/ 1894 'Fall Down a Pit Shaft at Eskett Mines'].

Appendix 5

Major Cumberland Mining Areas

The iron ore mines worked ore bodies that lay from Lamplugh, through Salter, Eskett, Parkside, Cleator and Cleator Moor, then through to Woodend and Longlands with off shoots of ore around Bigrigg, Moor Row, and on under Egremont to Haile. The ore beds are about eight miles long beside the road to Lamplugh, about one mile wide, and ten to thirty metres thick. At Cleator Moor the Montreal Mine became famous for uniquely raising coal and iron up number 4 pit- the black and red currants of Norman Nicholsons poem *Cleator Moor*.[131] The ore was about two thirds metal when purified, and one third rubbish.

One body of ore sat beneath Cleator Moor's St Johns church, under Montreal Street and across to Earl Street, and followed the cycle path toward Moor Row in a rough triangular shape. The ore was mined by Leconfield, Stirling, the Berrier Company, the Carron Company, Robertson Walker, and Dalzell from the High Street down to between the Jacktrees and Crossfield Roads.

At Crowgarth mine the ore lay in a seam 8 metre thick buried 24 metres under ground. It was reported as used up in 1829 having raised 20,000 tons a year between 1784 to 1810.[132]

Before 1974 the Furness peninsula was part of Lancashire, but since 1974 the area became part of the new Cumbria county, with the redundant iron mines at Askam, Lindal Moor, and Stank. In the south of Cumberland was a huge body of haematite at Haverigg and smaller amounts in Eskdale. The

---

[131] Norman Nicholson OBE in his early book of poetry about Cumberland, *Five Rivers* Faber and Faber 1945.
[132] William Parson and William White (1829), *History, Directory and Gazetteer of Cumberland and Westmorland with Furness and Cartmel*, republished by Michael Moon Beckermet, page 198, 1976

West Cumberland mines are commonly thought of as coal producers. But as well as iron ore other materials have been mined in smaller quantities in the area like lead, and graphite.

The coal mines follow the coal seams that run 20 miles north out of Whitehaven to Maryport then across almost to Wigton, and slope down ward and out under the sea. The coal seams are about 5 miles wide, and the eleven workable seams amount to about ten metres thick if added together in 700 metres thickness of other rocks. There is about 400 million tons of coal in the seams.

Appendix 6

Family Seats Around Moor Row in 1829[133]

A Family Seat is the main house for members of the two social classes known as aristocracy and landed gentry. The aristocracy are thought of as families that rule over people because their families always have done. An aristocracy is the rule of a few over the many, in the interest of all, justified by their supposed superior intellectual and moral abilities, generally demonstrated by their control over large amounts of property. They are considered to be noble in their behaviour, by avoiding work and living off the proceeds of their land which is worked by other people. Generally an aristocrat will be expected to be rich, well known, well connected to royal families, and in charge. Landed gentry, meanwhile, make their living by renting out their land and consequently live a gentile life of the landlord.

Both classes have a desire to be addressed by a title, and to preserve their title by handing it down to family members. These require having money, normally made from owning land. Social and economic class reflects unequal access to rights, resources, and power in society. It has a strong effect on to education, quality of education, and the type of work available to people. It affects who one knows, the extent to which those people can provide support with employment opportunities, political participation and power, and can even health and life expectancy.

The coveted titles occupy a league table of desirability:

Emperor; King; Queen; Prince and Princess; Duke and Duchess; Marquis and Marchioness; Countess and Count or Earl; Viscountess and Viscount; Baron and Baroness; Baronet and Baronetess or Dame; Knight and Dame; Lord and Lady of the Manor; Esquire; Yeoman; Husbandman; Serf; Servant; Vagabond; Slave.

---

[133] Compiled by William Parson and William White (1829), *History, Directory and Gazetteer of Cumberland and Westmorland with Furness and Cartmel*, republished by Michael Moon Beckermet, page 7, 1976.

Family Seats Around Moor Row In 1829

FAMILY SEAT	NOBLEMAN, GENTRY OR CLERGYMAN in residence 1829
ACRE WALLS HOUSE, WHITEHAVEN	Joseph Steel Esq
ARMATHWAITE HALL, COCKERMOUTH occasional residence	Sir Fred Fletcher Vane, Bt
BRIDEKIRK, COCKERMOUTH	Henry Tashmaker Thompson, Esq.
CALDER ABBEY, EGREMONT	Thomas Irwin, Esq.
CARLETON HALL RAVENGLASS	Joseph Burrow, Esq.
CLIFTON HOUSE WORKINGTON	Richard Watts, Esq.
COCKERMOUTH CASTLE, occasional residence	The Right Hon., Earl of Egremont
DERWENT BRIDGE END COCKERMOUTH	Major Humphrey Senhouse
DISTINGTON RECTORY	Rev. Henry Lowther
DOVENBY HALL COCKERMOUTH	Joseph D B Dyles, Esq.
GILGARRAN, WHITEHAVEN	Capt. James Walker, Royal Navy.
GILLFOOT, EGREMONT	Thomas Hartley, Esq.
GREYSOUTHERN, COCKERMOUTH	Joseph Harris, Esq.
HENSINGHAM HALL, WHITEHAVEN	Sir Joseph Senhouse, Knt.

Moor Row in 1891

The HIGH, COCKERMOUTH	Thomas A Hoskins, Esq.
HOLM ROOK, RAVENGLASS	Major Skeffington Lutwidge
HUTTON HALL	Sir Fred Fletcher Vane, Bt.
INGWELL MOOR ROW	Joseph Gunson, Esq.
IRTON HALL RAVENGLASS	Samuel Irton, Esq.
ISELL VICARAGE COCKERMOUTH	Rev Chpr Hilton Wybergh
LINETHWAITE MOOR ROW	John Lamplugh Raper, Esq.
LORTON HALL COCKERMOUTH	Raisbeck Luccock Bragg, Esq.
MORESBY HOUSE WHITEHAVEN	William Hartley, Esq.
MUNCASTER CASTLE RAVENGLASS	Rt Hon Lord Muncaster, Lowther Augustus John Pennington, 3rd Baron Muncaster
NAWORTH CASTLE CARLISLE	Rt Hon Earl of Carlisle, George Howard, of CASTLE HOWARD Yorkshire.
NETHER HALL WORKINGTON	Humphrey Senhouse, Esq.
ORMATHWAITE HALL KESWICK	Captain Joseph Dover.
PAPCASTLE COCKERMOUTH	Major Henry Skelton
PARK NOOK EGREMONT	Charles Parker, Esq.
PLUMBLAND RECTORY COCKERMOUTH	Rev. Edward Stanley

Family Seats Around Moor Row In 1829

PONSONBY PARSONAGE EGREMONT	Sampson Senhouse, Esq.
ROSE CASTLE CARLISLE	Hon Hugh Percy, Bishop of Carlisle
SPRINGFIELD BIGRIGG	John Ponsonby, Esq.
STEEL BANK WHITEHAVEN	James Steel, Esq.
TALANTIRE HALL COCKERMOUTH	William Browne, Esq.
VICARS ISLE DERWENT LAKE	Major-Genral William Peachy
WHITEFIELD HOUSE COCKERMOUTH	Joseph Gillbanks, Esq.
WHITEHAVEN CASTLE	Rt Hon Earl of Lonsdale, William Lowther.
WOOD HALL COCKERMOUTH	John Sanderson Fisher, Esq.
WORKINGTON HALL	Henry Christian Curwen, Esq.

Appendix 7

The Row on the Moor as built in 1891

Railways, roads, rivers, Terraces, and grand houses, built on mines.

The sketches below are based on Ordnance Surbey maps showing the buildings of Moor Row and surrounds of 1891. The oldest houses are the homesteads and grand houses, then the east side of Dalzell Street. The sandstone village was complete apart from the north east end of Penzance Street by 1898. Map 4 shows the post 1950s modern sprawl as cross hatched areas, although building had not started at the old railway yard as of 2023.

KEY

x1 Stirling Pit shaft.

x2 Postlethwaites mine shafts

x3 and **x4** Moor Row Mine shafts

x5 Sir John mine shaft

x6 Fletcher pit shaft

A allotment gardens

AH Alva House, office to Thomas Gavan Duffy MP

BS black ships

BM Ordnance Survey bench mark on Needless Bridge

Ch Methodist chapel

CH Crossfield House

CM Crossfield mine

CMM Cleator Moor mine

CS Crash site of traction engine from the road bridge

DC Dalzell crossing for railway

E Ehen Hall

F Flosh

FC Fisher Court cottages

FP Foot path lost under field

G Gutterby cottages

The Row On The Moor As Built In 1891

H Homesteads
HL High Lodge house
I Ingwell Hall
JH Jacktrees hospital
MM Montreal mine
MR Moor Row mine
P Park House
QB Quaker bridge
RC Rock crusher
RH Railway Hotel
RT Railway terrace houses
RY Railway yard
S Station
Sch School
Sh Shaw house
SH Scalegill Hall
SB Signal box remains
Sp Springfield House, Bigrigg
SP Signal Post, Moor Row
ST Station Terrace houses
StJ Saint John's church
StL Saint Leonard's church
TE Train explosion site

TM Site of Tin Mission for rail workers
VH Site of the Village Hall, built after 1900.
W Water well
Wi Site of Thomas Wildridge's home and gardens.
WM War memorial

Moor Row in 1891

Map 1: The Moor Row Neighbourhood of the 1890s.

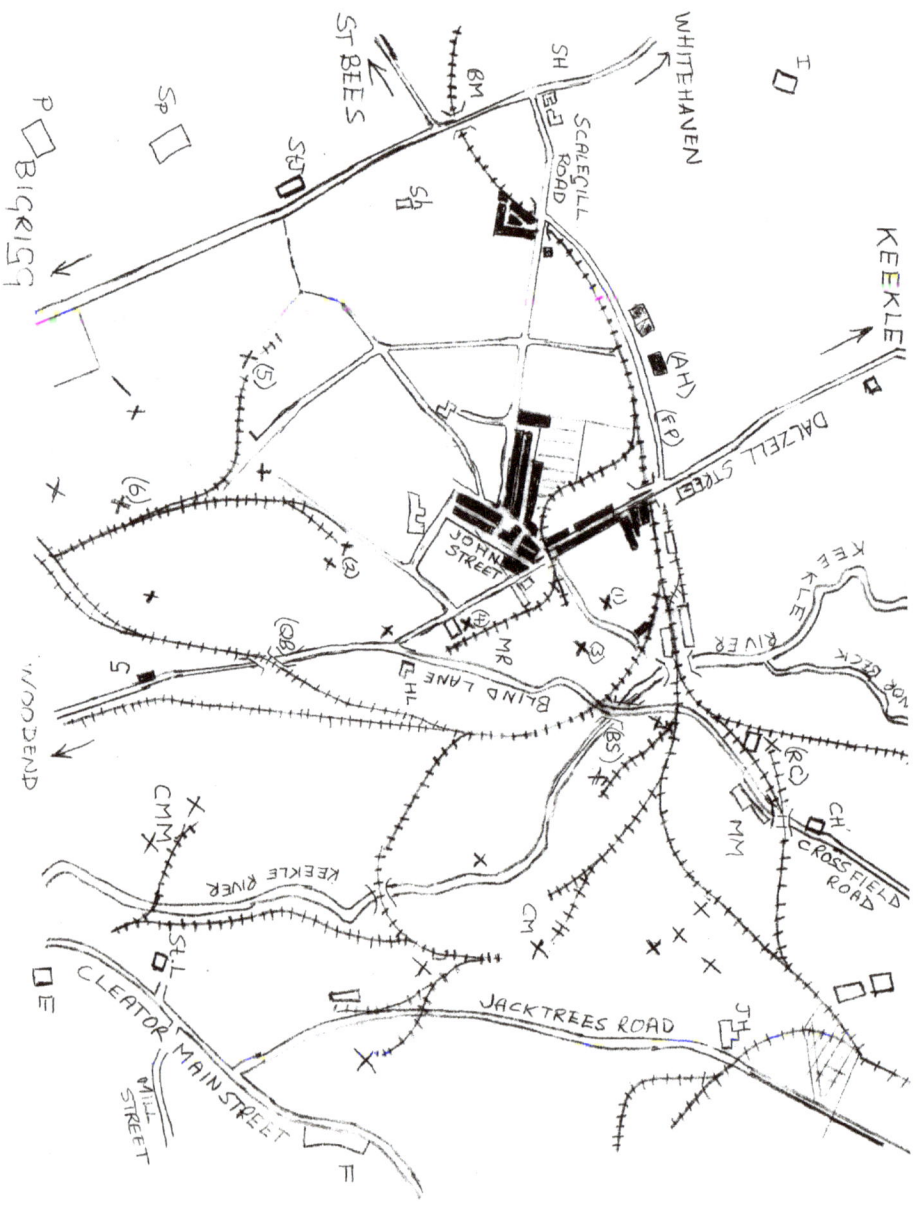

Map 2: The Moor Row Ribbon Development of the 1890s

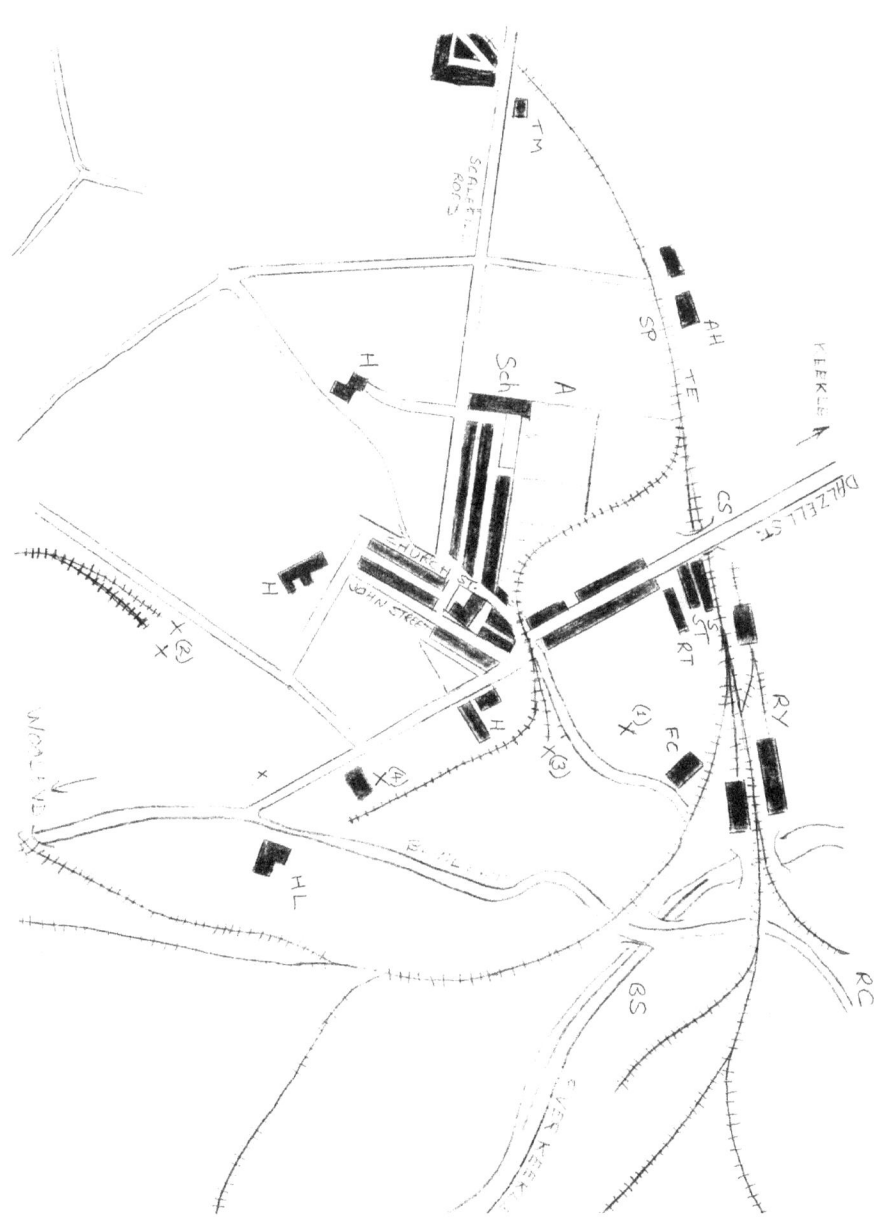

Moor Row in 1891

Map 3: The Moor Row Town Centre of the 1890s.

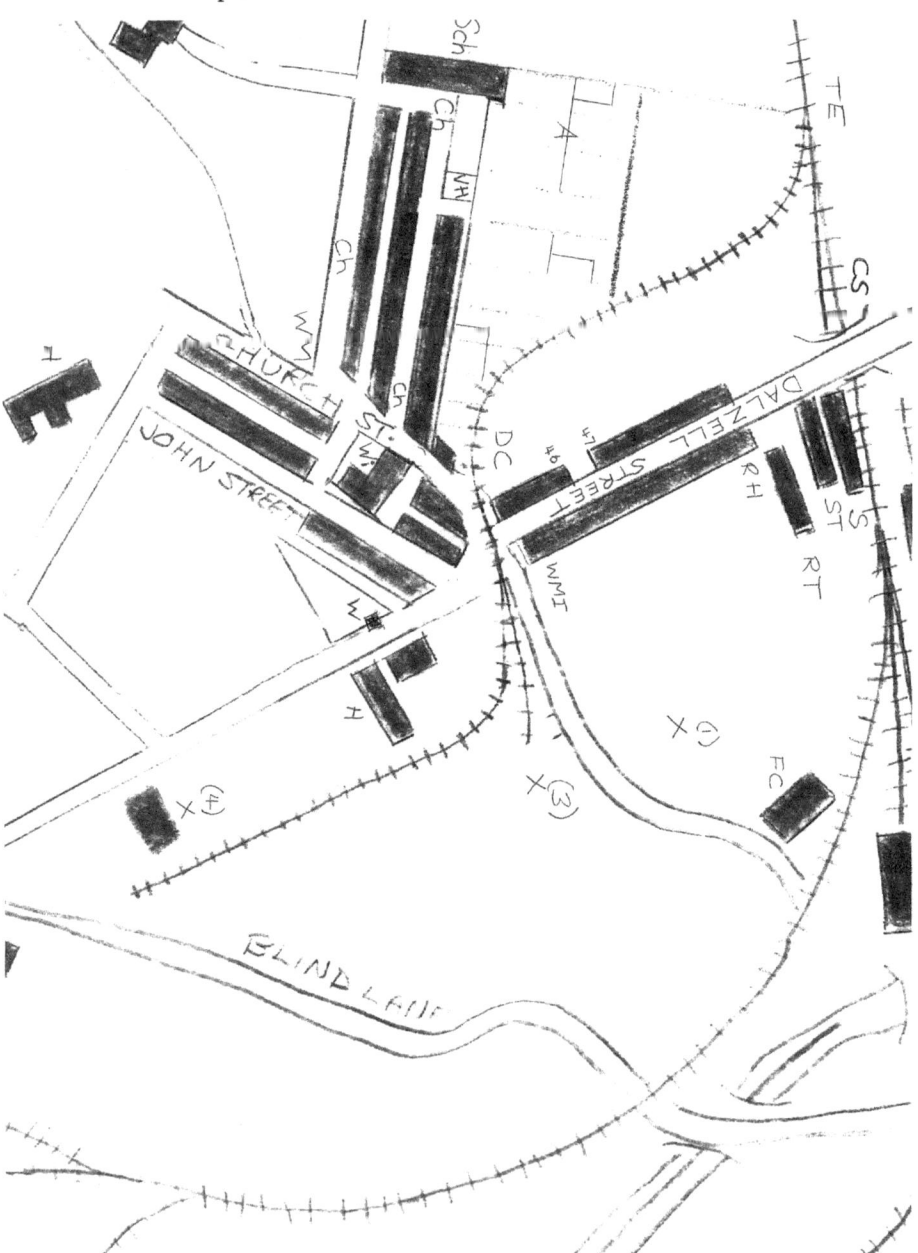

The Row On The Moor As Built In 1891

Map 4: The Moor Row Sprawl in 2023

References

Allen, R. C.(1979): *International Competition in Iron and Steel, 1850 – 1913, Journal of Economic History*, 39, 4, pp 911- 937, Cambridge University Press.

Edward Bains, (1824) *History, Directory and Gazetteer of the County palatine of Lancaster.*

Barber, R. (1976); *Iron Ore and After; Boom Time, Depression and Survival in a West Cumbrian Town, Cleator Moor 1840 – 1960*, York University and Cleator Moor Local Studies Group.

Beckett, J V (1982): *An Eighteenth Century Case History: Carlisle* Spedding 1738, Medical History, 1982, 26: 303-306.

Boyer, G. R.; *New Estimates of British Unemployment 1870 – 1913* The *Journal of Economic History, Vol. 62*, No. 3 (Sep., 2002), pp. 643-675 Cambridge University Press.

Bulmer, T & Co 1901: *History and Directory of Cumberland 1901* .Snape and Co., Preston.

Caine, C., (1916); *Cleator and Cleator Moor Past and Present*, Titus Wilson Kendal. Reprinted by Michael Moon 1973 and 1988, Beckermet and Whitehaven.

R. Colls (1987): *Pitmen of the Great Northern Coalfield: work, culture and protest 1790 – 1850*, (Manchester).

Cooter, R.J (2005) *When Paddy Met Geordie 1840 – 1880*, (Sunderland).

Crowe K., (1976). Thomas Burn Catherwood and the Medical Department of Wellingtons Army 1809–1814. Medical History; Vol 20 No 1

B Cubbon, P R Sandbach & C P Woollard, (2019) *The Red Earth Revisited.*

Moor Row in 1891

Daysh, G H J, (1938): West Cumberland (with Alston) *A Survey of Industrial Facilities*, Cumberland Development Council Ltd., Whitehaven.

G H J Daysh, (1945): *Memorandum on Cumberland With Special Reference to the Development Area,* Cumberland Development Council Ltd., Whitehaven.

Daysh, G H J, and Evelyn Watson (1951): *Cumberland With Special Reference to the West Cumberland Development Area,*: Survey of Industrial Facilities, Cumberland Development Council Ltd., Whitehaven.

M Dodd (2009); *The Story of Iron Ore Mining in West Cumbria.*

D R Hainsworth (1983): *The Correspondence of Sir John Lowther of Whitehaven 1693 – 1698,* Oxford University Press.

Huddleston, C. Roy and Boumphrey, R. S. ; *Cumberland Families and Heraldry*, Cumberland & Westmorland Antiquarian & Archaeol. Society.

Jewkes, J. & Allan Winterbottom, 1933: *An Industrial Survey of Cumberland and Furness*, Manchester University Press.

J Y Lancaster and D R Wattleworth (1977); *The Iron and Steel Industry of West Cumberland: an historical survey*, British Steel Corporation.

Mannix and Whellan, (1847): History, Gazetteer and Directory of Cumberland, republished Michael Moon Beckermet, 1974.

J D Marshall (1971); *Old Lakeland*, David & Charles: Newton Abbot.

J. D Marshall (1978);*Cleator and Cleator Moor: Some Aspects of their Social and Urban Development in the mid-19th Century*, Cumberland & Westmorland Antiquarian & Archaeological Society Transactions, Series 2, vol 78.

References

J D Marshall & J K Walton (1981) *The Lake Counties from 1830 to the Mid Twentieth Century* Manchester University Press, Manchester.

J. A. McKenna and Richard G. Rodger (1985) *Control by Coercion: Employers Associations and the Establishment of Industrial Order,* in The Business History Review, 59, 2, pp 203 -231

Oxford Economics, 2017: *The Economic Impact of Sellafield* Oxford England. https://assets.publishing.service.gov.uk/government/uploads/system/uploads/attachment_data/file/730958/The_economic_impact_of_Sellafield_June_2017_Oxford_economics.pdf

Parliamentary Papers (1844): Report of the Mining Commissioner, (592) 16.

Parson, W. and William White (1829), *History, Directory and Gazetteer of Cumberland and Westmorland with Furness and Cartmel*, republished by Michael Moon Beckermet, 1976.

Sugden, E H, 1897: *History of Arlecdon and Frizington*, Rev E H Sugden author, edited by Richard Byers 1997 Cockermouth.

Alice Thornton *The Autobiography of Mrs. Alice Thornton*, of East Newton, Co. York, Cited in Osborough, W. N. "Wills that go missing- the quest for the lost will of Christopher Wandesford, Lord Deputy of Ireland" in Reflections on Law and History Four Courts Press Dublin (2006).

W. W. Tomlinson, (1915) *The North Eastern Railway, its rise and development* Andrew Reid and Company, Newcastle.

Transport for the North, (2019): Strategic Transport Plan, Transport for the North, 4 Piccadilly Place Manchester, M1 3BN https://transportforthenorth.com/wp-content/uploads/TfN-final-strategic-transport-plan-2019.pdf

www.ingramcontent.com/pod-product-compliance
Lightning Source LLC
Chambersburg PA
CBHW041139110526
44590CB00027B/4067